RADICAL PHILOSOPHY

2.18
Series 2 / Spring 2025

Future skills? **Bill Cashmore**	3
Not normal but ordinary **Sita Balani**	10
The fascistisation of social reproduction **Verónica Gago**	23
Temporary autonomous friend **Sophie Lewis**	35
Dossier: Marina Vishmidt, 1976-2024	41
Crystal drills **Ray Brassier**	41
Against running in place **Zoe Sutherland**	44
Total art and mimetic subsumption **Daniel Spaulding**	53
Minor compositions **E.C. Feiss**	58

REVIEWS

Gillian Rose, *Marxist Modernism* **Rachel Pafe**	65
Gillian Rose, *Marxist Modernism* **Harrison Fluss and Benjamin Noys**	68
Aaron Schuster, *How to Research Like a Dog: Kafka's New Science* **Alexi Kukuljevic**	72
Jörg Später, *Adornos Erben [Adorno's Heirs]* **Jordi Maiso**	77
Cameron Abadi, *Climate Radicals* **Chris Dite**	82
Maria Chehonadskih, *Alexander Bogdanov and the Politics of Knowledge after the October Revolution* **Isabel Jacobs**	85
Alenka Zupancic, *Disavowal* **Rafael Holmberg**	92
Yuk Hui, *Machine and Sovereignty: For a Planetary Thinking* **Connor Eckersall**	96

Editorial collective
Brenna Bhandar
Victoria Browne
David Cunningham
Isabell Dahms
Marie Louise Krogh
Lucie Mercier
Robert Nichols
Hannah Proctor
Rahul Rao
Chris Wilbert

Engineers

CC BY-NC-ND
RP, Spring 2025

ISSN 0300-211X
ISBN 978-1-914099-07-6

Centre for Research in Modern European Philosophy

CRMEP BOOKS

Available as free ebooks direct from CRMEP or as paperbacks from Central Books

Institution
critical histories of law

Afterlives
transcendentals, universals, others

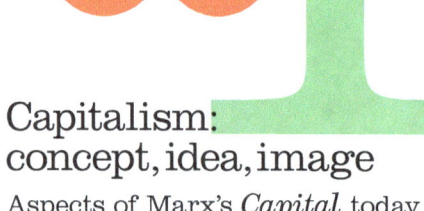

Capitalism: concept, idea, image
Aspects of Marx's *Capital* today

Vocations of the political
Mario Tronti & Max Weber

Thinking art
materialisms, labours, forms

Kingston University London

www.kingston.ac.uk/faculties/kingston-school-of-art/research-and-innovation/crmep/crmep-books

Future skills?

On the planned closure of the Centre for Research in Modern European Philosophy at Kingston

Bill Cashmore

On 26 February 2025, students of Philosophy, English and Creative Writing at Kingston University London received an email titled 'Proposed changes within Department of Humanities', sent on behalf of the Dean of the Kingston School of Art, Mandy Ure. In that email, the University revealed 'proposals to close the Department of Humanities', with English and Philosophy ceasing to take on new applicants, and Creative Writing moving to another department. Students were assured that our 'views will be a really important part of [the consultation] process.'

For staff at the Centre for Research in Modern European Philosophy (CRMEP) this was not a new experience. Four of them were part of the CRMEP when Middlesex closed it down in 2010, and accepted an invitation to move to Kingston later that year. It wasn't a novelty to students either: in early February 2024, we received a very similar email which initiated a 'Review of Philosophy programmes'. The Professors received another, different set of communications, at the same time as we did. As in the message sent in February of this year, it cited a decline in student recruitment, driven by a combination of government policy and market trends, as part of the justification for suspending applications to courses in Philosophy. In that case, the review was improvised at faculty level to judge the apparent 'viability' of Kingston's philosophy programmes. It is worth noting at the outset that recruitment to CRMEP's courses is in fact quite buoyant. A drop was certainly suffered after Brexit, when the number of students from the EU fell dramatically, but as of late February 2025, the MA courses had received 59 applications for 2025-26, and made offers to a large majority of them, mostly from overseas. Based on past experience, application numbers could easily have exceeded 100 by June. Meanwhile the CRMEP remains a central locus for research-based philosophical activities in the UK. Its public research seminars regularly attract scores of participants and remain the occasion for hours of animated discussion and debate; the most recent seminars, by two PhD students nearing the end of their dissertations, were on the philosophy of ecology and the concept of civil war. At the time of the proposed closure there were still 26 PhD students in Philosophy, despite the freeze on new applications that began a year ago. This is not, by any measure except that apparently adopted by Kingston's managers, a department struggling for recruitment or significance.

The purpose of this piece is to make clear how students at CRMEP understand this closure of our Centre. Last year's review, and its implied conclusions, were contested and resisted by both staff (who raised grievances regarding the secrecy of the process) and students at CRMEP; eventually, the review failed to publish any conclusions and passed over into a 'period of reflection'. We counted this, broadly, as a victory. Our campaign was one of strategic de-escalation, focusing on points of weakness within the university's review procedure, to locate points where the process, represented as natural and necessary, was in fact far more contingent, dependent as it was on the choices of a few individuals. Our campaign did not go public at the time. This is because we judged that our resistance would be more effective if we resisted incorporating ourselves within wider discourses around the funding of the humanities in Higher Education, which are increasingly beholden to a myth of inevitability, believed by those who support, and those who oppose, the marketisation of universities.

This year, however, the proposed cuts came against a background of increased preparedness on the part of the Kingston University administration. In particular, the administration emphasised an alleged need to make £20 million worth of cuts over the course of two years, the majority of which are this year to be made in the Humanities and Social Sciences (though £10m was saved last year, by other means). As a result of the scale of the proposed cuts, and the nationwide cuts to so many similar programmes and departments across UK universities in the last year, we felt that a more public campaign was more likely to be successful this time around, with the rationale that Kingston's reputation would suffer if their plans were made public. This is especially the case in light of the University's unwillingness to confirm that they would allow our Professors to teach out the students already signed up for Masters and Doctoral courses, bearing similarities to a case at the University of Essex, recently ruled upon in favour of the students by the Office of the Independent Adjudicator.[1] The precedent set by this judgment might lend some cause for optimism, however limited, for students threatened by cuts to their departments.

Despite the similarities between the 2024 and 2025 situations, there has been a notable change in discursive emphasis from the Kingston administration. There is a growing emphasis on teaching something called 'Future Skills', oriented around the belief that universities ought to change their teaching in order to adapt students to 'the world of work'.[2] Each year since 2021, when the Future Skills agenda began, a report has been commissioned by Kingston University to justify the shift toward such skills and, by implication, away from the education on which universities have historically focused. The skills were determined by a survey of 'business leaders' in the UK. Nine such skills were identified, and are now the focus of Kingston's compulsory Future Skills modules for all undergraduate students: (1) creative problem solving, (2) digital competency, (3) being enterprising, (4) having a questioning mindset, (5) adaptability, (6) empathy, (7) collaboration, (8) resilience and (9) self-awareness.[3] On the face of it, of course, none of this seems particularly at odds with an education in the humanities or social sciences, certainly not in a research environment in which most students will be locating and compiling resources predominantly digitally. As such, it might appear surprising that it is the plan to cultivate these skills that prefaces the announcement of the proposal to close the Department of Humanities.

The surprise is, however, explained in part by the more recent turn towards a specific vision of the future for which students at Kingston are now being prepared, in part by a brute matter of the reduction of costs. Regarding the latter, Kingston University's plan is to shift the teaching of Future Skills away from humanities academics. These are not just skills communicated through other modules, but are specific modules, now necessarily at least 25% of all taught courses. This comes along with Kingston's removal of all optionality in the provision of modules, so that students will no longer have any possibility for specialisation based on their interests. Future Skills modules are to be outsourced to an education consultancy firm called GradCore. Those teaching the modules no longer need to be qualified as academics in the way in which those currently working at universities are. In short, Future Skills has become the label under which the cost of teaching is reduced – de- and re-professionalised – with a branding of innovation and future-preparedness, while its real content is the provision of university-level certification (complete with university-level tuition fees) without university-level teaching.

Perhaps the more significant element is this former aspect, the vision of the future assumed by Future Skills. In the most recent Future Skills report, supported by JP Morgan, the focus shifts markedly towards Artificial Intelligence (AI), and its 'rapid development' and 'exponential growth', according to Kingston's Vice-Chancellor.[4] This goes as far as to say that the 'modern ... world of work' can *already* be described as 'AI-first'. This claim is not substantiated. In general, the evidence of the need for universities to pivot towards the teaching of AI is based on the expressed opinions of business leaders about what they expect could happen to techniques of labour, though there is, of course, no reason to suspect that business leaders are likely to be accurate in their predictions, or to understand their consequences. In fact, what is perhaps most surprising about the research structure of the report is that there is no account of exactly what must change in response to this alleged growth in AI, nor what this growth actually is. The only example cited is Open AI's Chat-GPT, whose place seems rather under threat as the ecological impact of LLM-based Artificial Intelligence is at last attracting scrutiny,[5] and the emergence of international competition threatens the viability of stock market investments in large American AI firms.[6]

Back in 1735, James Wyatt invented the spinning machine and proclaimed its autonomy from labour in its ability to 'spin without fingers'. As Marx notes, however, it was not without labour: donkeys supplied the power to these machines, and there remained a labour, albeit now further alienated from the labour process, of feeding and keeping these donkeys.[7] Throughout its history, of course, capitalism has invented machines which revolutionise the labour process so as to increase its productivity. Marx called this 'the intensification of labour', which appropriates more labour-time per hour by virtue of the labour-time crystallised within the machine.[8] But perhaps more importantly, it allows for the reduction in the cost of the labour-power employed in the use of the machine, since the apparent simplification of the labour process allows for a reduction in the cost paid for that labour, by virtue of the reduction in the socially necessary labour time required in its reproduction – although the 'moral and historical factors' in the determination of the value of a certain period of expenditure of labour-power are, at least in part, determined by what are determined as a worker's 'so-called necessary wants and needs', the minimum living standard acceptable to individuals according to their position in society.[9] Moreover, the centralisation of the cooperation of workers in machines allows for the simplification of labour such that the labour of one individual takes the place of that of many others. What does not change, however, is the structure of production itself, which remains, as we might expect, dependent on wage-labour and private property. Just as the cost of reproducing the labour of a single stable hand and a donkey is far less than that of sewers, the cost of reproducing workers who can operate an AI chatbot is less than that of workers who were previously doing this

A man with a wooden leg carrying arms and legs in a basket; representing the relation between the whole and its parts in Aristotelian logic. Engraving by L. Gaultier, ca. 1613. Wellcome Collection.

work 'themselves':

> The whole system of capitalist production rests on the circumstance that the worker sells his labor-power as a commodity; the division of labor narrows his labor-power to the point where it becomes a very particular competence in handling a specialized tool; then, when his tool falls prey to a machine, the exchange-value of his labor-power immediately vanishes along with its use-value. The worker becomes unsellable .... Some members of the working class are rendered superfluous by machinery: they are turned into a population that capital no longer needs to valorize itself.[10]

Here, the vanishing of the value of labour-power is an outcome of a process that was meant merely to be an increase in the productivity of that very labour-power.

Those 'moral and historical factors' in the determination of the value of labour-power, which appeared at first to be independent of the process of production itself, now appear influenced by this process as workers are reduced to the mere operators of tools, and then, eventually, as the work is made autonomous of the workers themselves, the value of their labour-power is abolished, and more and more of the population are rendered 'useless' – made not just unemployed, but *unemployable* in the fullest sense. Those remaining in employment are then forced to accept lower wages, a logic that was explicitly stated by Kingston University, of its own students, in a now-deleted update to the new university website:

> Hiring one of our graduates offers you: Affordability:

> Maximum enthusiasm and a fresh approach *at a lower salary*.[11]

On the same page, Kingston praises the diversity of its student body, which, combined with this message, seems to imply that one of the uses of Kingston University to alleged employers is the provision of a diverse (read: non-white) student body willing to accept low wages. This is the nature of contemporary capitalism's increasing dependence on the creation and management of surplus populations, a result of the increasing accumulation of capital rendering labour unemployable. As such, there is an ever-growing portion of the population for which capital has no use other than as an effectively infinite supply of labour upon which it can draw in order to suppress wages.[12] Viewed in this context, the discourse of Future Skills begins to appear as the rendering unemployable of workers in the present on the basis of an expectation about the developments of technology in the future, an unemployability that ought to be fought, by universities, with an abolition of teaching in the humanities. In this sense, Future Skills is no doubt an attempt to secure the continued existence of universities like Kingston, but it makes this claim in a discourse in which all of capital's goals have already been taken for granted.

In 2022, the Future Skills report asks for integration of its language by politicians, including the creation of a Future Skills council modelled on the Creative Industries Council which 'will focus on how to solve the workforce skills challenge and the roles of [sic] government, industry and education can each play.'[13] This is part of a general attempt to remove the educational significance of universities, which is the heart of the Future Skills initiative, expressed in the attempt to change their position within the state. In response to the lack of funding to Higher Education, the proposed move is to

> align universities' teaching and learning missions with economic growth and innovation by moving them out of the Department for Education to the Department for Science, Innovation and Technology and Department for Business and Trade.[14]

The guiding motive, therefore, seems clear: to abolish any distinctly educational function of universities in favour of increased integration with capitalist 'innovation'. The structure of this subjectifying function, determining that universities need to be reformed for future employability, is thus an operation of this 'future' upon the present, in order to lower the cost of labour-power. As noted in the open letter written and signed by CRMEP students, opposition to the humanities is frequently justified both in terms of the lack of its use-value in the production process and its left-political content, especially as it relates to queer, feminist and anti-racist politics.[15] In the United States, years of campaigning, under the guise of promoting 'free speech' in universities, led by figures such as Christopher Rufo and James Lindsay, has now legitimated a general attack on universities as promoting an ideology threatening to the American state; all elements of the academy are now deemed compromised by the pervasive influence of, among other things, critical theory and feminism. As is well-known, the Trump White House issued an executive order 'ending radical and wasteful government DEI programs',[16] now extended to include a list of words which, if included in research, will result in a review of their funding grant, including 'race', 'LGBTQ' and even 'female'.[17] While the assault on the universities is not limited to research which might be deemed to have left-political content, nonetheless this research is deemed *especially* useless in the face of the metric of employability.

It is therefore with the utmost concern that we should read the promise of Kingston's Future Skills reports to invent a new 'employability metric that will support start-ups, entrepreneurs and industries'.[18] Insofar as the concept of the future is indexed with regard to possibility, by virtue of the fact that, at least socially speaking, no one knows what will occur, we have what Reinhard Kosseleck calls the 'horizon of expectation': the set of experiences deemed possible.[19] So not only is the meaning of the future everything that is possible, it also, by determinative negation, includes that set of experiences deemed *not* possible. The horizon of expectation, however, is not exactly the future, it is not just those events that have not yet occurred, but it is the future-in-the-present, the temporal meaning of the future felt as that towards which we are moving in time. Kant's critique of prophesy is useful here, since the horizon of expectations always makes some claim about what is possible, and we see how subjection functions through the narrowing of this horizon:

> We can obtain a prophetic historical narrative of things to come by depicting those events whose *a priori* possib-

ility suggests that they will in fact happen. But how is it possible to have history *a priori*? The answer is that it is possible if the prophet himself occasions and produces the events he predicts.[20]

Such prophesies are made, Kant argues, by politicians who claim to take humans ' "as they are", but this "ought to read" as we have made them by unjust coercion, by treacherous designs which the government is in a good position to carry out.'[21] We might say that the descriptions of AI and future technology in Kingston's Future Skills reports are not strictly speaking predictions, but rather *prophesies* that, in their acceptance as prophesies, make themselves true. The moment of resistance to this domination of the future lies, then, in the rejection of these prophesies as the outcomes of merely positive claims about how employment will change. An order is always given in these prophesies. Every prophesy contains an imperative.

This prophetic logic has already operated quite concretely in our own situation: the figure of £20m was generated out of a shortfall on projected earnings after student recruitment for 2024-2025 was not as high as projected. This was not a deficit, not money lost in the present, but money lost on a projection. The perverse logic of financial prophesy operates this way: a prophesy is made, often unattainable, and the failure to realise this prophesy justifies the (re)institution of a particular state of affairs, particular relations of power. We can now read the moral content in such financial projections: the prophesy *ought* to have been made true, and the fact that it was not justifies social change to bring us closer to this perfected state. Kant's analysis holds true today, insofar as the prophetic mode is a strategy of instituting states of affairs desirable to those who hold power. However, prophesies no longer make themselves true, on the basis of taking humans 'as they are' and not as they ought to be; our capitalism's prophesies make themselves false, taking humans as (capital thinks) they 'ought to be', not as they are.

So it matters rather little whether the devaluation of the humanities comes from apparently benign prophets of technological progress, or from more explicit denouncement of their research as a kind of subversive agenda. The claim, uniformly, is that we, as a society, cannot waste time and money on education. At least, this is the case for the greatest portion of society, those in the precarious position of being rendered 'unemployable', and thus surplus. The same fate, we should note, is unlikely to befall universities like Oxford or Cambridge, whose endowments for the humanities are apparently beyond threat. This casting of the humanities as always proximate to unemployability is, at least in part, because its education does more than simply prepare people, primarily young people, for employment. It involves the attempt at a communication of something which is not yet understood by those being educated, something that Friedrich Schlegel called the 'incomprehensible' moment in the transmission of an idea.[22] There is something in education that Peter Osborne, the Director of CRMEP and a former editor of this journal, has noted is absolutely in opposition to *training*.[23] Whereas the latter involves the cultivation of a skill for the purpose of the improved fulfilment of some task, the former always involves changing the understanding of those being educated. Educational difficulty, then, is a symptom precisely of the fact that a certain idea is not easily comprehensible against a particular background. This was intended, in that lecture, to clarify the importance of difficulty in the teaching of any idea. But it might here be generalised to the fact that the humanities, especially philosophy, often deal with initially incomprehensible ideas and texts at almost every moment of their teaching, and so strictly speaking this incomprehensibility means their value always exceeds their use, their employability. It is this resistant quality of education itself, that it lingers within the face of incomprehensibility, which is threatening to a worldview based solely on training, since there remains a moment in this education which *is constitutively unemployable*, and affirms this precisely as its value. Education in this sense remains genuinely transformative and threatens the authority over the future to which any discourse of Future Skills makes claim, not only in its ability to call into question the concepts invoked in making this claim, but also in this structural fact of education itself.

I have elected not to speak too much of the value of CRMEP specifically here, since those reading this journal will require no convincing of the significance of the content of the research that is undertaken here, with or without direct familiarity with its research and teaching. However, if I might speak personally for a moment, it is this commitment to what is difficult, unincorporateable, unemployable, that makes CRMEP often feel to me like a singular reprieve from a Higher Education system that seems less and less about education. Texts which have, in the UK, often been discounted precisely on account of their incomprehensibility to the dominant modes of philosophising, retain a place at CRMEP not simply because they can be justified by their conversion into a digestibly Anglophone 'Continental Philosophy', but because the hermeneutic density of these texts, their persistent incomprehensibility, reflects thought's non-enclosure of the real. Our collective bafflement in the face of these texts, over and over again in libraries and seminar rooms, is perhaps what remains their most important quality, that they might teach us the value of unemployability, and the terror of a world that would be easily understood.

Bill Cashmore is a PhD student in Philosophy at Kingston University. Her work is on the challenge posed to philosophy by the Black Radical Tradition, particularly concerning the concepts of value, narrative and relation.

Notes

1. The OIA ruled that these students had a 'legitimate expectation to be taught by an expert they signed up to the course to be taught by'. Leigh Day Solicitors, 'Adjudicator rules in favour of students left in academic limbo after African history course was axed', 20 February 2025, https://www.leighday.co.uk/news/news/2025-news/adjudicator-rules-in-favour-of-students-left-in-academic-limbo-after-african-history-course-was-axed/.
2. Kingston University, 'Future Skills at Kingston University', https://www.kingston.ac.uk/about/future-skills.
3. 'Future Skills'.
4. Kingston University, 'Future Skills – The Kingston Approach', 2023, 1, https://assets.kingston.ac.uk/m/2f62cc1612165a88/original/20231129Future-Skills-Report-2023.pdf.
5. Sophie McLean, 'The Environmental Impact of ChatGPT: A Call for Sustainable Practices In AI Development', *Earth.org*, 28 April 2023, https://earth.org/environmental-impact-chatgpt/.
6. Kelly Ng et al, 'DeepSeek: The Chinese AI app that has the world talking', *BBC*, 27 January 2025, https://www.bbc.co.uk/news/articles/c5yv5976z9po.
7. Karl Marx, *Capital, Volume 1* [1872], trans. Paul Reitter, 2nd edition (Princeton: Princeton University Press, 2024), 342.
8. Marx, *Capital*, 377.
9. Marx, *Capital*, 144.
10. Marx, *Capital*, 397.
11. https://www.instagram.com/p/DHq505kN$_L L/$, 24 March 2025, emphasis added.
12. William Robinson, 'Global Capitalism's Extermination Impulse', *The Philosophical Salon*, 19 August 2024, https://www.thephilosophicalsalon.com/global-capitalisms-extermination-impulse/.
13. Kingston University, 'Future Skills - League Table', 2022, https://assets.kingston.ac.uk/m/43626c23951b08fb/original/2022Future-Skills-League-Table-2022V1.pdf, 22.
14. 'Future Skills - The Kingston Approach', 26.
15. E-flux Notes, 'Open Letter from CRMEP Students & Researchers on Kingston University's Proposed Closure of the Department of Humanities', 5 March 2025, https://www.e-flux.com/notes/658933/open-letter-from-crmep-students-researchers-on-kingston-university-s-proposed-closure-of-the-department-of-Humanities.
16. The White House, 'Ending Radical And Wasteful Government DEI Programs And Preferencing', 20 January 2025, https://www.whitehouse.gov/presidential-actions/2025/01/ending-radical-and-wasteful-government-dei-programs-and-preferencing/.
17. Karin Yourish et al. 'These Words Are Disappearing in the New Trump Administration', *New York Times*, 7 March 2025, https://www.nytimes.com/interactive/2025/03/07/us/trump-federal-agencies-websites-words-dei.html.
18. 'Future Skills - League Table', 22.
19. Reinhardt Koselleck, *Futures Past: On the Semantics of Historical Time*, trans. Keith Tribe (New York: Columbia University Press, 2004).
20. Immanuel Kant, 'The Conflict of the Faculties', trans. H.B. Nisbet, in *Political Writings*, ed. H.S. Reiss (Cambridge: Cambridge University Press, 1991), 177.
21. Kant, 'Conflict', 178.
22. Friedrich Schlegel, 'On Incomprehensibility', trans. Peter Virchow, in *Lucinde and the Fragments* [1800] (Minneapolis: University of Minnesota Press, 1971), 259.
23. This was a class, given as part of Kingston's 'Teaching and Learning in Higher Education' module.

Not normal but ordinary
Living against the culture wars
Sita Balani

Gender has become a key ideological, legislative and organisational concern for the hard right on a global scale. The social acceptance and political representation of trans people and gender non-conformity joins questions of racial diversity, gender equality and climate change as hallmarks of what the right, in their attempt to reshape the political terrain into a series of interlocking 'culture wars', refer to as 'woke' ideology. While many dismiss the culture wars as a politics of distraction, a way to divert our attention away from deteriorating economic conditions, here I work from the premise that this is only their surface utility. Rather, questions of culture, identity and nation function as legible and charged images through which experiences of infrastructural decline, loss of status and fear of unknown futures are negotiated. In their capacity to condense complex historical processes into powerful moral panics, the culture wars function as a tool for sewing together otherwise diverse constituencies, scrambling older political categories through what William Callison and Quinn Slobodian have described as 'diagonalism'.[1] Inhabiting the space opened by the crumbling of state welfare and social infrastructure, as well as left institutions (unions, political parties) in retreat, diagonalism allows for constituencies to be peeled off through appeals to nativism, nature or family values. In diagonalist politics, wellness gurus, former Marxists, critics of pharmaceutical companies, gun-toting libertarians, anti-abortion activists, Christian evangelicals, Muslim manosphere influencers, incel podcasters, trad wives, astrologers and more, can find common cause.

The culture wars are propelled by the logic of the zero-sum game. As I have written with colleagues elsewhere, 'If you believe the fulfilment of another's desire is always at the expense of your own, then someone else's gain, however minor, will always be your loss'.[2] In Britain, this language of loss is used to conjure a mythic 'white working class' who are understood to have been 'left behind' by globalisation at the hands of metropolitan elites. In the familiar telling of this story, racialised outsiders – the illegal immigrant, the Muslim, the Black youth – are the immediate beneficiaries of the establishment's betrayal of the innocent white native. In recent years, we've seen this racial story spawn a gendered variant. What Sivamohan Valluvan, Amit Singh and James Kneale have described as the 'distinctly contemporary nationalist narratives of decline and grievance' have been remade as a story about the threat of 'gender ideology' to proper, dignified gender roles, the family and the nation.[3] The culture wars thus frame any increase in relative power and dignity of women or trans people as a threat to men, cisgender people and the national polity as a whole.

The culture wars, however, are not merely a rhetorical exercise but a legislative one. To give some examples: in 2020, the Hungarian parliament imposed new legislation preventing legal gender recognition for trans and intersex people, and updated the constitution in terms drawn from culture war rhetoric, stating: 'Hungary shall protect the right of children to their identity in line with their sex at birth, and shall ensure an upbringing in accordance with the values based on our homeland's constitutional identity and Christian culture.'[4] In the US, there has been a wave of anti-trans legislation, taking aim at participation in sports in schools, gender-affirming healthcare and use of public toilets. In Britain, new legislation has been introduced to prevent access to puberty blockers for young people. At the time of writing, dozens more bills are working their way through national legislatures around the world.

One key legislative and rhetorical focus is on trans women's access to women-only spaces (hospital wards, changing rooms, toilets), but the same gendered anxieties also animate the claim that masculinity is under attack by 'woke' ideology. As Felix Del Campo observes, in the hard right discourse, the 'appreciation of "masculine virtues" as fundamental pillars of an organic, ethnically homogeneous political community appears alongside anti-genderism'.[5] This concern with 'remasculinisation' is spearheaded by right-wing digital content producers, such as Andrew Tate, Jordan Peterson, Sneako and others who have grown large followings on YouTube and TikTok and via messaging apps and alternative video streaming platforms such as Rumble. As Haslop and colleagues observe in their research on Tate, 'platform affordances, such as visibility, anonymity, algorithmic politics, echo chambers, as well as the "disinhibition effect" … enable misogyny and anti-feminist activism to thrive in digital spaces'.[6] As digital life becomes entangled with all aspects of the social, the 'manosphere' – as these circuits of networked misogyny and aggrieved masculinity are known – has set up shop in the cultural mainstream. Teachers, for example, regularly attest to the reach and prominence of manospheric misogyny in the classroom, and to the knowing use of its provocative idiom by teenage boys.

According to Judith Butler, in this right-wing ecosystem, gender has come to function as a 'phantasm', condensing economic and social anxieties. This 'catchall phantasm' allows for gender non-conformity to be figured as 'a threat to all of life, civilization, society, thought' by those who wish to return us to a 'patriarchal dream-order'.[7] The identification of this phantasm offers a useful means of apprehending the psychic dimension of moral panics. However, this approach suggests that 'gender' is foremost in most people's minds and is the site of dramatic social conflict. In this article, I suggest that the tools of cultural studies might allow for us to grasp the ways in which 'everyday informal life'[8] can run counter to this mediatised phantasm. Butler's notional solution to the culture wars is to issue what Brock Colyar has described as 'a boilerplate call for collective action by the oppressed'.[9] While this would certainly be a welcome political development, it nonetheless continues to work on the assumption that people's political attachments are already clearly defined and that the task at hand is merely to unify them. I propose that instead we need to attend to the ways in which the culture wars may fail to recruit willing soldiers, the ways in which people live against the paranoid logic of *ressentiment*. I am concerned with the contexts in which the psychic pull of identity – and gender identity specifically – may recede in the face of social connections that run along other channels, stake other claims, or offer other pleasures. First, I'll suggest a turn from queer theory to cultural studies as a conceptual move away from a critique of 'norms' towards an assessment of the 'ordinary'. I'll then consider 'conviviality' as a useful theoretical tool, before considering the work of two contemporary photographers, Roman Manfredi and Mahtab Hussain, and their depictions of masculinity.

The problem with normal

The watchword of the culture wars project is 'normal'. The so-called 'left behind' – the abandoned denizens of Britain's deindustrialised heartlands – are understood as 'normal'. But normal does other work too. Professor Eric Kaufmann, author of *Whiteshift* and representative of this hard right project's academic flank says, 'If politics in the West is ever to return to normal rather than becoming even more polarized, white interests will need to be discussed.'[10] Normal here stands for the restoration of an uncontested majoritarianism. And, of course, in their slogan 'adult human female' tweeted ad nauseam and emblazoned on t-shirts, key transphobic lobby group, the LGB Alliance, are staking their own claim to 'normal'. In this, they align perfectly with political elites, including former UK Prime Minister Rishi Sunak whose 2023 Conservative Party speech insisted, 'we shouldn't get bullied into believing that people can be any sex they want to be. They can't. A man is a man and a woman is a woman – that's just common sense.'[11] Normal here is not figured as mundane or resigned, but as dignified, rational, natural and scientific.

In this context, I want to suggest that queer theory's critique of norms might be more of a hindrance than a help. When 'normal' becomes the explicit framing of a hard right project, there is little to be gained from observing the limitations of 'normal' – it is precisely these limitations that are being claimed and defended. Further, queer theory's critique of normativity has itself become incorporated into the 'anti-gender' movement through its attack on gender studies departments. In this context, we must revisit queer theory to assess its limitations as well as its purchase on the culture wars. As Robyn Wiegman and Elizabeth A. Wilson put it, 'normativity has come to stand as the negative force against which the field [of queer theory] crafts its self-definition'.[12] This approach has been highly generative: queer theory has been able to turn its gaze on the habits, rituals and practices of heterosexual or cisgender life, for example in Michael Warner's influential 1999 attempt to think queer politics of and beyond gay marriage.[13] In turning our attention to what is already peculiar or idiosyncratic but naturalised in the world of public hetero-performance, the tools of deconstruction were used to shake the apparently stable foundations of heteronormativity. Nonetheless, this approach regularly reasserted the subversive nature of queer lifeworlds and practices, setting up intellectual habits that cannot gain a meaningful purchase on our current conjuncture.

One can trace this intellectual development through the 1990s and 2000s. The rise of gay liberalism – with successful campaigns for gay marriage, adoption rights, and broad social acceptance in many countries – gave a new energy to queer studies, providing it with a clear foil. In the wake of these legislative shifts, and despite the uneven and novel sexual politics of hard right regimes, the radical/liberal dichotomy has proven hard to shake. A critique of Reagan's or Thatcher's explicit homophobia was supplanted by an aversion to the way that their neoliberal worldview had reshaped gay life. Thatcher and Reagan's political successors dropped the explicit homophobia – politicians such as Tony Blair, Barack Obama and David Cameron actively embraced gay rights while maintaining neoliberal economic and social politics – and queer theory riled against what it called 'assimilation'. This approach, however, depended on a view of heterosexual and cisgender life as something quite fixed, with norms regulated by state power.

Such a static view of heterosexual and cisgender life is unsustainable. The British state's interest in enforcing 'norms' seems increasingly limited to the use of neglect, in the form of austerity and managed decline, or through carceral technologies of arrest, detention or deportation. These technologies are largely agnostic on the matter of the sexual practices of most citizens. Put in other words, state institutions simply don't care if you're polyamorous or into BDSM, and there's a fair chance your colleagues don't either. It's clear that hetero-life is in a state of significant flux: divorce rates are at a record high; in 2023, *New York Magazine* devoted a whole issue to polyamory; and app-based dating is now the norm. Recent years have seen the rise of non-monogamous dating apps, highly commercial content about and commodities for kink practices, and a broad range of pornography that is easily available. There is a growing market to profit from the 'alternative' sexual habits of putatively heterosexual people, for example the dating app Feeld (annual turnover of £39.5 million),[14] the e-commerce site Love Honey and a range of parties and sex clubs. Further, the currency of inclusion, whether we conceive of that as seductive or coercive, loses some value when there is little in the way of functioning state structures in which to be included. The antinomies of assimilation and antinormativity can no longer hold. In many ways, straight life now appears to be modelled on the habits of late twentieth-century gays as much as gay life can now inhabit the scripts of heteronormativity. And though there has been an increase in street homophobia and transphobia in Britain, this should not be seen as a 'return' to the bad old days – these are bad new days with their own, specific challenges. As such, different methods of critique and analysis, beyond those offered by queer theory, are needed.

The ordinary and the convivial

I suggest that one way to approach questions of gender and sexual identity in this conjuncture is to bracket queer theory's lexicon of normativity, assimilation, radicalism and subversion. The tools of cultural studies offer a way to break out of this critical deadlock, paying attention to the ways in which, however powerful 'normative' representations appear, people may not live according to their scripts. The gap between mediatisation and everyday life is an important one, which is not to discount the dazzling power of the culture industry but to insist that it is not totalising. The Marxist habits of cultural studies – which insist on the importance of constrained agency, situated creativity, and attentiveness to cultural production in everyday life – are useful here. After all, we make *meaning* in circumstances we've inherited too.

As Willis insists, the creative, symbolic work undertaken in everyday life through the codes of dress, gesture and style are communicative: if we attend to these codes, we may be able to locate prefigurative political possibilities.

The lineage of cultural studies I draw on here can be traced to the Centre for Contemporary Cultural Studies (CCCS) at the University of Birmingham in the UK, first directed by Richard Hoggart, and later by Stuart Hall. Interdisciplinary from its inception, cultural studies brought the method of close reading from literary study to bear on social practices – on how people dress, dance, speak and move. Drawing on history, sociology and anthropology, as well as continental theory, this approach focalised an 'ethnographic sensibility' even when its practitioners did not directly engage in ethnographic research.[15] It is this sensibility that I attempt to inhabit here, by turning in the next section to an auto-ethnographic anecdote from my own life, as well as Amit's Singh's recent ethnography of an East London kickboxing gym.[16] Importantly, in both its interdisciplinarity and its concern with mediation, cultural studies resists making a fetish out of the empirical or abandoning the theoretical in favour of the purely descriptive. As such, ethnographic insights are opportunities for further theorisation and analysis.[17] Sexuality has been somewhat under-theorised by cultural studies, but its tools remain available to better understand the role of gender, sexuality and sexual politics within specific conjunctures. This approach is concerned with ideology, but more attuned to the Gramscian language of hegemony. Unlike in queer theory, Foucault enters the field as a more minor player here. Nonetheless, a microphysics of power is articulated and examined in the granular specificity of a more sociological register. Taking this approach allows us to attend to the texture of everyday life as it is lived in the teeth of impersonal forms of domination. In other words, how do people live not only *in* but *against* the culture wars?

In returning our attention to vernacular, offline spaces of sociality, we can find ways to relegate questions of normativity to the background. Here I draw on what Paul Gilroy refers to as conviviality: the everyday experience of people living cheek-by-jowl – not the choreographed multiculturalism of corporate diversity nor a self-conscious celebration of 'difference', but the 'messy complexity of social life'.[18] In a similar vein, Ash Amin theorises the 'civilities of indifference to difference'.[19] Gilroy and Amin are not suggesting that people live without friction or even conflict, but that there's a broader reticence towards identity categories than official discourse would suggest. The demotic ethic of 'live and let live' – perhaps now reconfigured as 'you do you' – may endure beyond the purview of algorithmic capture. Gilroy suggests that conviviality might point to vernacular modes of 'refusing race and salvaging the human'.[20] My concern is less to extend the theory of conviviality beyond race, in order to apply it to sexuality or gender. Rather, I want to suggest that within the convivial arrangements that persist in contemporary Britain, there is already a certain openness to gender and sexual diversity. This is not to say there isn't tension, friction, violence or outright homophobia and transphobia. As Luke de Noronha reminds us, 'conviviality only proves generative, conceptually and politically, because it points to the messy, contingent and often unremarked ways in which people live together and care about one another *against the odds*, in societies structured by racial division and hierarchy'.[21] I take up this insight to suggest that a certain indifference to sexual and gender diversity can be located in everyday life, despite the rising power of transphobic rhetoric and legislation.

Developing this interest in the messy and contingent, my contention is that conviviality should be viewed as distinct from the rise of institutional inclusion or corporate diversity. Conviviality is not to be located in the institutional etiquette of pronouns in your email signature, rainbow lanyards or Equality, Diversity and Inclusion training. Indeed, my wager is that some of these institutional practices, in their shallowest forms, intensify the divisive rhetoric of the culture wars. One must note that these practices take shape and are experienced against the gleaming visual sphere of the culture and social industries, in which racialised and gender-diverse models and actors are increasingly prominent, to the rage and resentment of the hard right. My suggestion is not that their objection is a reasonable or progressive one, rather that the experience of seeing new figures take centre stage in the dreamscape of television, film and advertising is being metabolised through a hard right narrative of usurpation. Further, while the ordinary racialised or queer person cannot be held responsible for corporate aesthetics and their unpredictable consequences, we may nonetheless wish to take a more sceptical and more vigilant view of our 'inclusion': something rather more serious than 'assimilation' is at stake.

In light of these limitations, we must turn our attention to the spaces beyond institutional capture – the interstitial leisure spaces of pubs, parks, gyms and shared residential worlds, not least what remains of social housing. There is much to be gained from attending to how people navigate offline spaces beyond the purview of the HR department. Further, in turning to photography (as I will do shortly), we can take stock of representation not as a reflective medium but as a constitutive one. As Kobena Mercer puts it,

> once culture is understood as the medium in which social subjects 'make sense' of their lived experiences in language, discourse, and other symbolic codes that determine shared perceptions of reality, then representation gains primacy as a first-order activity in which identity is itself a production that constructs the positions from which we interpret and act in the social world.[22]

If we pay attention, therefore, to the spaces in which gendered identities play out beyond or against the hyperbolic, phantasmic constraints of the culture wars, we may be able to locate practices from which we can construct a more robust counter-imaginary.

In the gym

A few months ago, I took a lunchtime class at my local boxing gym. I've boxed on and off, fairly casually, for the past seven years. The boxing gym closest to my house is a well-established family-run space – its primary aim is to train fighters and it uses recreational classes and personal training to generate an income. As such, a cross-section of the local community uses the space, both adults and children, albeit for slightly different purposes, some aiming to become competitive fighters, others to get fit and learn a new skill. The gym smells of sweat and leather. Under the thrash and thud of people smashing the heavy bags, music plays through the speakers rigged up in the corners of the cavernous space. What tunes depends on the coach – happy hardcore, jungle, afrobeats, grime. When you get to know both the coaches and the timetable, you can guess whose phone is plugged into the speaker before you come through the door. This lunchtime, only my second or third visit to this gym, I noticed that someone in the class was definitely a kid – maybe a young teenager, 12 or 13, perhaps. I suppressed my concern that perhaps he ought to be in school and got on with warming up. Then there was someone else, a boxer whose age I couldn't pin down. Maybe also a child? Baby-faced and stocky, but with a self-possession that seemed unlikely in a youth. As someone of a similarly modest height, I ended up sharing a bag with him. We ran through the drills and he was kind and patient, taught me how to slip his shots (which were much quicker and stronger than mine), touched gloves with me between rounds, and performed all the conventional habits of training together. At the end of the class, he packed his stuff up and got on a motorbike. That seemed to resolve the question – he was not a child, after all.

The following week, I was warming up with a skipping rope on the gym floor, my mind wandering. The same boxer came over. Sorry, maybe this is a weird question, but how old are you? I laughed. 36, I said, a bit ruefully. *No way! I swear I thought you were a kid. Like a teenager. But you're all tatted up*, he said, gesturing to my inked shoulders and calves. *So I figured, you couldn't be a kid*. I told him the confusion had been mutual, and we both laughed till the drills started. This happens to me sometimes and is a common experience for butch dykes, as well as many other gender non-conforming people. As we left, after class, touched fists, he said *next time, bro* and I realised that perhaps some confusion still remained. We had been unable to discern very much about each other – not age, perhaps not gender, certainly not race. The channels of recognition, if we are to use this term, were full of static. Though we have come to view misrecognition through the lens of violence, erasure or domination, here I suggest something else is at play. Though we were not transparent to each other, nor even legible through the grammar of identity, we were nonetheless engaged in a complex practice of co-operation, mutual respect, trust and humour.

I have similar interactions – in which conviviality is not dependent on transparency – with some regularity, but I have selected this example because its setting is instructive in its contradictions. Singh's recent ethnographic study makes some suggestive interventions on boxing gyms as having a particular set of affordances – both atomising and collectivising. On the one hand, Singh observes the neoliberal logic underpinning the gym's ethos, in which the insistence that fighting is a meritocracy leads to the derision of those who cannot perform the requisite bodily functions. Equally, the gym is a space in which the usual identity markers – race, gender – can fall away, undermined by the immediate, visceral experience of training, sweating, fighting. He suggests that there's a strong sense of responsibility towards each other in these spaces, observing, 'You have to rely on your training partners for sparring, therefore requiring mutuality and respect.'[23] Singh borrows from Butler, as well as Pierre Bourdieu and Gilroy, to theorise shared choreographies of the body as 'carnal convivialities'. He observes that 'Sparring requires one to lend one's body – with its vulnerability as well as its training and skills – to another, in service to mutual improvement.' In this space, the identity of 'fighter' can supersede the markers of race, sexuality and gender.

The theory of normativity's coercive power to shape our interactions does not seem to offer much analytic purchase on how people are able to shrug off the impositions of identity under particular circumstances, such as in boxing gyms. And to deem these instances 'radical' or anti-assimilationist threatens to undermine precisely what makes them worthy of our interest. In these ordinary interactions, in which gender, race, even age, are held in abeyance, we can discern some compelling possibilities. Of course, as Jasbir Puar and David Eng note, an understanding of the provisional nature of identity is already built into the foundations of both Marxist and queer theory. Eng and Puar observe that both Marxist and queer theory 'underscore the fact that the subject is necessarily opaque to itself and eminently imbricated in a web of social relations and responsibilities, a self with primary ties to unknown and unknowable others'.[24] What cultural studies offers is a method for attending to the particular locations, methods and practices through which this web of social relations passes and is shaped.

My aim here is not to obscure or deny the continuing operations of prejudice nor the institutional operation of discrimination. Conviviality is not a theory of the colour- or gender-blind liberal subject. But if we overstate the extent to which the culture wars are hegemonic, we run two risks. The first is a kind of nihilism in which we are unable to grasp political opportunities or excavate resources for hope. The second is that we risk imagining political subjects as both flat and coherent. Instead, my argument works from the premise that there is likely a productive disjuncture between the kinds of digital content that people consume and the way they behave in their interactions with others. Not in all instances: we know, for example, that some participants in incel subcultures commit acts of violent, indeed, fatal misogyny. But we ought to be more circumspect in our assumptions about how the ambient culture war rhetoric shapes everyday interactions.

Roman Manfredi

WE/US by Roman Manfredi is 'an intergenerational photography and oral history project that celebrates the presence of butches and studs from working-class backgrounds within the British landscape'.[25] Though the framing of identity and representation is central – the subjects share an identity and have been chosen on this basis – the work itself points us to other interpretations. Manfredi shoots the subjects in places that matter to them. It is the suburban, small town or semi-rural locations that capture my attention and seem to offer an interesting riposte to the culture wars binaries. As Valluvan points out, 'the distinction that remains perhaps most defining of this need to cleave today's political ructions into neatly irreconcilable camps, one aloof and idealistic, the other rooted and earthy, is the one that is drawn between metropolitan cities and provincial towns'.[26] By insisting on lesbian life with some shared style, energy, tone and warmth in a variety of locations – rural, metropolitan, semi-urban, industrial, post-industrial, provincial – Manfredi makes these neat distinctions untenable.

This habit of associating queerness with the urban is politically promiscuous – after all, the 'coming out' story that has dominated queer life for decades is usually one of escape to the big city. But coming out assumes one has the choice of being 'in' the closet to begin with. For many butches and studs, an affiliation with masculinity predates sexual identity. Indeed, for some, queer sexuality is identified by playground homophobes or anxious adults before they had the chance to work it out for themselves. In *Stone Butch Blues*, for example, a foundational text of butch and trans identity, the protagonist is the subject of homophobic bullying and violence before she herself is able to identify her sexual or gender identity.[27] While many of the oral history interviews talk of the first visit to a gay bar or the call of urban queer life, the images themselves depict a rather different relationship with place, one that retains a set of deep attachments to mixed spaces not defined by identity. The greater focus in the oral histories on activism and discrimination – as well as parties, relationships, pride, power, sport and family – speaks to the ways in which a more ethnographic approach (as in the images) can yield something distinct from interviews. As Manfredi said in HUCK magazine, 'I wanted to place us in [residential] environments because we're often only ever photographed in our underwear, in a sexualised or eroticised way, or in clubs. We do that ourselves and we need to claim that and it's fine but you don't expect to see us in an everyday setting.'[28] By shooting the subjects in locations that matter to them, in 'everyday settings', the images draw attention to identity as always unfolding *somewhere*, tethered to time and place, rather than in the frenetic non-place of digital life.

Laura, Wembley, London © Roman Manfredi

It is no coincidence that Manfredi's exhibition was co-curated by the path-making photographer Ingrid Pollard. Pollard's work comprises both portraiture, documentary and landscape, focusing on rural spaces. Notably, her most famous work *Pastoral Interlude 1982-1987* has been consistently subjected to a kind of paranoid interpretation, assuming that its depiction of black walkers in the English countryside is one of anxious unbelonging. In a 2022 interview in the *Guardian*, Pollard observes,

'People immediately say ... It's about alienation. It's about white landscape, Black people. [...] It gets bashed into whatever shape people want to put it in.'[29] In the face of reductionist interpretations of her work, Pollard insists that these images are a commentary on the construction of place; racism is present – undeniable and explored – but has no monopoly on meaning or experience. Pollard's artistic vision coalesces beautifully with Manfredi's work. The exhibition offers a powerful rejoinder to the story of English decline, masculinity in crisis and provincial-metropolitan antagonism that has dominated life in Britain in recent years. It says, there are other masculinities: Other Englands too.

That the masculine subjects in question are mostly women gives the work an unusual capacity to challenge expectations around class, place and belonging. The story of Britain's deindustrialised hinterlands, 'left behind' by metropolitan elites was essential to the Brexit project and the nationalist convulsions that continue in its name. As observed, this narrative is a gendered one. It is assumed that Britain's working class men have been usurped by gender radicals, antiracists and their protectors in the political elite. Gender non-conformity is viewed as the tip of the 'woke' spear. It is to this story that these striking images offer a quiet but powerful rejoinder. Masculinity in crisis seems a little silly in the face of Manfredi's photographs. What crisis? The idea that men are wondering how to be men appears a little melodramatic. The photographs appear to say, *Try being a dyke. Try having tits and a face tattoo. Try street harassment.* Worked-on bodies – familiar with the regime of macros and protein shakes – are presented alongside but never in comparison with softer frames. There is a frank, confident sexuality on display, in which age and race are held within that sexual confidence, not in spite of it. Youth is sexy; so are wrinkles. The subjects wear suits or sports bras, leather jackets or sherwanis. There is no 'normal' here, no centre and margins.

Though a small number of masculine dykes have joined the ranks of 'gender critical feminists', butches and studs experience similar social penalties to many trans and non-binary people. As one of the oral history interviews observes, 'Those lesbians that have somehow decided it's not okay to be trans are the same lesbians that would have told me that it wasn't okay to be butch.' These shifting antipathies reveal the culture wars to be a labile and enduring presence, in which queer life is shaped by – and is by no means immune from repeating – broad social prejudice. The speaker notes that this anxiety about gender displayed by 'extreme political lesbians' revolved around questions of *style*: 'they wanted people to wear knit-your-own trousers and dance without a rhythm'. In its embrace of swagger – as well as the 'dykes and faggots against transphobia' badge I bought at the exhibition gift shop – the exhibition makes clear where it forges its alliances. There is a palpable sense of ease and political expansiveness, with an organic diversity that feels genuine, unforced. The composition as a series allows a productive mediation between group and individual, never letting one stand in for the other, nor allowing them to become antagonistic. The title *WE/US* offers a method for this mediation. As pronouns become highly politicised, it's refreshing to be reminded that we already have a gender inclusive language of collectivity, there for the taking: We; Us.

Mahtab Hussain

Manfredi's photographs share a striking compositional similarity with Mahtab Hussain's series, *You Get Me?*[30] Hussain's first body of work, *You Get Me?* was inspired by his own experiences of growing up in Glasgow and then Birmingham as a young Muslim man. The series, which took nine years to complete, is an intimate engagement with masculinity, self-esteem, social identity and religion in a multicultural society. Shot between 2008 and 2017, its subjects face high unemployment and racism. In these years, the 'War on Terror', with its violent policing, surveillance and infiltration of British Muslim communities, reshaped the lifeworlds of working-class British Muslims. From 2015 onwards, the controversial Prevent agenda – which sought to infiltrate the social and cultural lives of British Muslims – was put on a statutory footing with the passing of the Counter Terrorism and Security Act. This legislation compelled public sector workers (in schools, hospitals, social services and so on) to report service users they felt were 'at risk of radicalisation'. Prevent disproportionately impacts both men and Muslims, with leaked Home Office documents naming 'British Muslims, particularly males aged 15–39' as the scheme's target.

This conception of Muslim masculinity as threatening or dysfunctional has long roots in the British national imaginary, with lurid stories about Muslim men animating the archive of Britain's colonial rule in South Asia, North Africa and the Middle East. In contemporary Britain, however, it is Pakistani and Bangladeshi men who are most often invoked as troublesome Muslim folk devils, associated with misogyny, violence and cultural insularity. Since the 2010s, stories about 'Muslim grooming gangs' have been a consistent source of fascination and a key recruitment tool for the hard right. While a longer engagement with the facts of organised sexual exploitation is covered elsewhere and beyond the scope of this article, it is useful to note the particular confluence of place, race and gender in the cynical repetition of these stories. While sexual abuse is endemic across society, the 'grooming gangs' captured the nationalist imagination precisely because they could be used to evidence the abandonment of Britain's towns and cities by the metropolitan elite, acting in defence of predatory racial outsiders.[31] Though Hussain's work does not make explicit reference to the moral panic surrounding 'grooming gangs', his photographs nonetheless offer a powerful rejoinder to the construction of Muslim masculinity as violent or threatening.

Like Manfredi, Hussain is concerned with capturing the texture of the lifeworlds from which the subject emerges. Though some of Hussain's images are closer to documentary, with the subjects eating or sleeping, in many, the subject looks directly into the camera. As in Manfredi's images, there is an open, frank sexuality here. As Helen Trompeteler observes, the photographs deploy three-quarter length composition, with the subject in the centre of the frame, a representative mode familiar from formal Western portrait painting. Hussain deploys this mode in a novel fashion, as all of the images are in a landscape mode to allow for a greater balance between sitter and setting.[32] As in Manfredi's work, location is of tremendous significance here, with the textures of quotidian residential architecture (the deep orange-red brick walls of houses in Birmingham's Sparkhill or Small Heath, for example) given formal weight beyond functioning as 'background'. As in WE/US, dialogue between photographer and sitter was key to this work, and Hussain quotes from his interlocutors at length in interviews and in the exhibition's accompanying book.

Comparing these two exhibitions yields other com-

Black hat, black glove and bling © Mahtab Hussain, *You Get Me?*, 2012

pelling possibilities too. Queers and British Asians are often assumed to be insular, defined by idiosyncratic attachments, outside of the mainstream. More acutely, these are communities so often assumed to be antagonists, with South Asians – and specifically Muslims – cast as uniquely homophobic. This was a key dynamic in Britain as the meteoric rise of gay rights became intertwined with the domestic and international politics of the 'War on Terror'. If we read these exhibitions together, however, this homonationalist framing can fall away. The subjects in these two exhibitions may not know each other, but they are engaged in a choreography of the body in which they might implicate each other through the way they dress, move, carry themselves. In other words, they are all engaged in the repertoires of masculinity. As Jack Halberstam said in *Female Masculinities*, 'although we seem to have a difficult time defining masculinity, as a society we have little trouble in recognizing it'.[33] Reading these images in dialogue, their similarity suggests a shared set of references, aesthetics and gestures.

In these images, bravado, fronting, cockiness, swag is its own pleasure, and offers pleasure to the viewer too. These butches, boys, studs and men have style. They pull their caps low, keep fades fresh, pour whole pay cheques through needles into tattoos that refuse the bourgeois demands of respectability. There is an extravagance at play, sometimes borrowing from hip hop culture's heavy jewellery, sportswear and branding. In a photograph titled 'Black hat, black glove, and bling' the displacement of the character of the sitter into these accessories highlights the constructed, composite nature of masculine style. The sitter's beanie is pulled low, shading one eye, and his heavy chain is caught in his teeth. The ostentation of his pose is provocative and playful, highly sexualised yet its implications are unclear; does the chain in his mouth signify force or docility? The cast of his gaze, up through his eyelashes, adds to the ambiguity of the image, in which femininity and masculinity cannot always be differentiated. Similar aesthetic modes are at play in Manfredi's image titled 'Gideon' taken in East Farleigh, Kent. The sitter, astride a motorbike, has a face tattoo on their right temple, the word 'FERAL' inked just under their hairline.

Yet this claim is an ironic one; there is a softness to their pose, their mouth forming more of a pout than a sneer. Their figure is framed by lush foliage, blue skies, fluffy clouds. The masculinities in these images are marked not by their distance from femininity but by the theatricality with which strength and vulnerability are patterned.

Gideon, East Farleigh, Kent © Roman Manfredi

If the pleasures of style – ludic, creative, cheeky, knowing – can be admitted and enjoyed, they may offer some protection from the seductions of the militarised, paranoid, crude and violent masculinities circulating via the social industry's predatory algorithm. They may, too, offer some respite from the concern that masculinity is intrinsically 'toxic', to use the language drawn from a rival plane of the digisphere. Rather, attention to the expressive possibilities found in dress, gesture, voice and bearing may be a point of productive connection shared across gender identities and sexed bodies. The shared masculinity is one of a working class at some ease with Britain's multiracial composition. Perhaps also one at greater ease with gender diversity than we might imagine. This is particularly significant in a time in which the question of English masculinity surfaces in political debate as an anxious, fractious, paranoid thing, a thing on which so much rests – not least, we are led to believe, the dignity of the nation. The culture wars assume a beleaguered masculinity as well as an aggrieved whiteness. Neither seem especially significant here.

Though imagined to inhabit different worlds, these photographs tell a more complex story. The spaces of working-class life are often shared, and Britain's towns, villages and housing estates encompass a more relaxed diversity than the culture wars would have you believe. Though portraits of individuals, these images are also depictions of a set of convivial possibilities. They say: *This pub is my local, I box in this gym, I know these streets, I live on this estate, I buy chips from this takeaway, I am from here*. The subjects look outwards. They return our gaze. But they also invite us in, allowing us to see these spaces as convivial ones, not owned by any particular group. It is easy enough to imagine Manfredi's subjects and Hussain's subjects crossing paths, sharing spaces, touching gloves in the gym, catching the same bus, reaching for the same pair of AirMax in the shop, chatting at the barbershop. While we cannot assume all of their interactions would be seamless, free of misapprehension, resentment, prejudice or confusion, equally, we can see in these ordinary shared lifeworlds an alternative to the anxious, fractious presumptions of the culture wars.

Indifference to difference?

The story of the culture wars divides the world into a series of binaries; yet the tools of deconstruction, on which queer theory has been so reliant, offer little to our analytic arsenal. While, of course, the binaries of 'woke'/normal or metropolitan/provincial must be challenged, to reveal their cross contamination or interdependence is insufficient. Rather, we must look for the ways in which everyday life might already furnish us with possibilities beyond confected culture wars antagonisms. In turning my attention to masculinity here, as a vector of convivial possibilities, I attempt to build on the insights of Les Back and Shamser Sinha who draw our attention to the 'paradoxical co-existence of both racism and conviviality in city life'.[34]

First, I have selected exhibitions which insist that provincial, suburban and rural spaces also contain convivial possibilities. Second, I pause on spaces, methods and aesthetics associated with masculinity's excesses, with bravado, arrogance, homoeroticism and aggression. For this reason, boxing gyms recur in the ethnographic research as well as in both exhibitions, as potent examples of locales in which characteristics associated with mascu-

Young boy, white boxing gloves © Mahtab Hussain, *You Get Me?*, 2010

line excess can be productively channelled into healthy, convivial modes of engagement. While the culture wars are propelled by digital 'content', boxing is resolutely analogue, requiring presence, focus, cooperation and discipline. Though content relating to fitness is a key genre in the 'manosphere', the actual practice of training or fighting relies on a kind of humility in which 'carnal convivialities' become possible. Of course, as Andrew Tate's career as a professional kickboxer attests, not everyone will take up these possibilities. Nonetheless, gyms are a regular feature of suburban areas and small towns as well as urban spaces, offering a way to view conviviality as the preserve not of regions but of practices. In this way, the provincial/metropolitan divide recedes in significance.

In their work on desi pubs, Valluvan, Singh and Kneale suggest that these South Asian-run boozers have become multiracial social spaces. This is particularly significant because the pub is claimed by melancholic nationalists and culture wars opportunists as a symbol of white English decline. According to these writers, the desi pub offers an opportunity to dislodge this story. But, they say, 'that dislodging is undertaken undemonstratively, where there is not a particularly pointed attempt to fill in that displaced, vacant normativity with an alternative minoritarian equivalent around which the assumed subjectivity and symbolism of the space is to be exclusively staked'.[35] To take up this analysis in regards to Manfredi and Hussain, we might argue that they depict masculinity without a normative referent, without exclusionary claims. There is not a critique of normative, bourgeois, white or indeed 'male' masculinity here – one doesn't appear to be needed. There is no attempt to say 'this is the true masculinity'. What is shown here is profoundly ordinary, but need not be normal.

While a concern with the quotidian rather than the normal offers an alternative to culture wars antagonisms, the portrait mode allows for the ordinary to also be the site of dignity and meaning. Here, working class masculinities often rendered provocative, threatening or dysfunctional are elevated by their depiction within the form of fine art photography. Butch and stud masculinities have historically been rendered failures to achieve proper womanhood. Further, as discussed, Muslim men have become sites for racialised fantasy and nationalist scapegoating. In this context, the particular form of the portraits is notable: in almost all, the sitter meets the eye of the audience. As Hussain observes, 'It was the gaze that I was drawn to, that direct look at the audience. For me, that was power in its purest sense, knowing that someone was going to look at you, judge you, but you too were able to judge them.'[36] Holding eye contact is often understood as an expression of masculine power. Here the sitters look out, they hold our gaze, but they are also objects of the gaze, the looked at, the desired. This experience of direct eye contact, of the gaze, has some interesting implications for thinking about conviviality. Scepticism about conviviality often centres on the way it has often been taken up in relation to fleeting encounters in public space. Critics suggest these kinds of encounters tell us relatively little about how people actually live relationally. In portrait photography, however, the fleeting encounter is expanded: one can contemplate the art work for a prolonged period, and the sitter never looks away.

To ask viewers to engage with working-class masculinities as sites of grace, composure, sensitivity and style is a powerful antidote to the culture wars. These images offer a method for refusing the fiction of the normal citizen, the innocent dupe of the metropolitan elite. At its heart, this story relies on a certain conception of the hapless working class subject, whose stolid social conservatism is under threat by the pernicious forces of wokery. This smug embrace of ignorance is nowhere more apparent than in the blunt pseudo-science of 'adult human female' or the banal resentments of anti-feminist backlash. These exhibitions suggest we can counter this cultivated ignorance by attending to the complex reality of everyday interaction. Travelling at ground level, rather than in the stratospheric fiction of newspaper columns or social media's grubby resentments, we can attend to the vernacular ways in which people refuse the culture wars. The ordinary convivial socialites of certain rural, suburban and inner city spaces may contain within them a plausible antidote to a rising inchoate fascism. This antidote is not coded in the language of celebration, nor even the statist grammar of recognition, but in a kind of collective self-confidence, relaxed in the face of other ways of being. It is perhaps in this breezy indifference to difference that we may find the resources to uproot our own analytic habits.

Sita Balani is Senior Lecturer in English at Queen Mary University of London and the author, most recently, of Deadly and Slick: the Sexual Life of Race in Britain *(Verso Press, 2023).*

Notes

1. William Callison and Quinn Slobodian, 'Coronapolitics from the Reichstag to the Capitol', *Boston Review*, 12 January 2021.
2. Gargi Bhattacharyya, Sita Balani, Dalia Gebrial, Adam Elliott-Cooper, Kerem Nisancıoglu, Kojo Koram, *Empire's Endgame: Racism and the British State* (London: Pluto Press, 2021), 163.
3. Amit Singh, Sivamohan Valluvan and James Kneale, 'A Pub for England: Race and Class in the Time of the Nation', *European Journal of Cultural Studies* 28:1 (2024), 165.
4. Blanka Vey, 'How trans people became Hungary's latest target', *Open Democracy*, 17 May 2023, https://www.opendemocracy.net/en/5050/hungary-anti-trans-homophobic-legislation-gender-recognition/.
5. Felix del Campo, 'New culture wars: Tradwives, bodybuilders and the neoliberalism of the far-right', *Critical Sociology* 49:4–5 (2023), 691.
6. Craig Haslop, Jessica Ringrose, Idil Cambazoglu and Betsy Milne, 'Mainstreaming the Manosphere's Misogyny through Affective Homosocial Currencies: Exploring How Teen Boys Navigate the Andrew Tate Effect', *Social Media + Society* 10:1 (2024), 2.
7. Judith Butler, *Who's Afraid of Gender?* (London: Allen Lane, 2024), 6.
8. Paul Willis, *Common Culture: Symbolic Work At Play In The Everyday Cultures Of The Young* (Abingdon: Routledge, 1999), 98.
9. Brock Colyar, 'Gender, Troubled: Judith Butler's Culture War Misfire', *The Drift* (5 March 2024).
10. Eric Kauffman, *Whiteshift: Populism, Immigration and the Future of White Majorities* (London: Penguin, 2019), 371.
11. 'Pride organiser invites PM to event after speech', BBC News, 6 October 2023, https://www.bbc.co.uk/news/articles/c0kx52587k1o.
12. Robyn Wiegman and Elizabeth A. Wilson, 'Introduction: Antinormativity's queer conventions', *differences* 26:1 (2015), 5.
13. Michael Warner, 'Normal and Normaller: Beyond Gay Marriage', *GLQ: A journal of lesbian and gay studies* 5:2 (1999), 119–171.
14. 'Feeld's Turnover Soars to £39.5 Million, Doubling Since Last Year', CGB, 9 September 2024, ht-

tps://cbg.com.cy/feelds-turnover-soars-to-39-5-million-doubling-since-last-year/.

15. Luke de Noronha, 'The Conviviality of the Overpoliced, Detained and Expelled: Refusing Race and Salvaging the Human at the Borders of Britain', *The Sociological Review* 70:1 (2022), 167.

16. Amit Singh, *Fighting Identity: An Ethnography of Kickboxing in East London* (Abingdon: Routledge, 2022).

17. See de Noronha, 'The Conviviality of the Overpoliced' for a productive discussion of conviviality, ethnography and theory.

18. Paul Gilroy, *Postcolonial Melancholia* (New York: Columbia University Press, 2005), 16.

19. Ash Amin, 'Land of strangers', *Identities* 20:1 (2013), 1–8.

20. Paul Gilroy, 'Never Again: Refusing Race and Salvaging the Human', Holberg Prize Lecture, 4 June 2019, https://holbergprize.org/events-and-productions/holberguken-2019/holbergforelesningen-never-again-refusing-race-and-salvaging-the-human/.

21. de Noronha, 'The Conviviality of the Overpoliced', 160.

22. Kobena Mercer, 'Stuart Hall and the Visual Arts', *Small Axe* 19:1 (2015), 80.

23. Singh, *Fighting Identity*, 31.

24. David L. Eng and Jasbir K. Puar, 'Introduction: Left of Queer', *Social Text* 38:4 (2020), 6.

25. For more on the exhibition, see: https://www.romanmanfredi.com/weus.html.

26. Sivamohan Valluvan, 'Cosmopolitanism in the "provinces"', *Soundings: A Journal of Politics and Culture* 80 (2022), 115.

27. Leslie Feinberg, *Stone Butch Blues* (Ithaca, NY: Firebrand Books, 1993).

28. Megan Wallace, 'Striking portraits that celebrate working class butch and stud identity', *Huck Magazine* (6 June 2023).

29. Ashish Ghadiali, '"People want me to say I'm alienated": Ingrid Pollard on the myths of art, race and landscape', *The Guardian*, 20 March 2022, https://www.theguardian.com/artanddesign/2022/mar/20/ingrid-pollard-myths-art-race-landscape-photography-interview-mk-gallery.

30. For more on the exhibition, see: https://www.yougetme.info/

31. For more on organised sexual violence and its exploitation by reactionary nationalists, see Ella Cockbain and Waqas Tufail, 'Failing Victims, Fuelling Hate: Challenging the Harms of the "Muslim Grooming Gangs" Narrative', *Race & Class* 61:3 (2020), 3–32.

32. Helen Trompeteler, 'Portraiture as Question: Reflections on "You Get Me?"', September 2017, https://www.yougetme.info/essay-portraiture-question-reflections-get/.

33. Judith/Jack Halberstam, *Female Masculinity* (Durham: Duke University Press, 1998), 1.

34. Les Back and Shamser Sinha, 'Multicultural Conviviality in the Midst of Racism's Ruins', *Journal of Intercultural Studies* 37:5 (2016), 518.

35. Singh, Valluvan and Kneale, 'A Pub for England', 13.

36. Mahtab Hussain interviewed by David Campany, Aperture Blog (2017), https://davidcampany.com/mahtab-hussain-interview-david-campany/.

All content now accessible …
radicalphilosophy.com

The fascistisation of social reproduction

Verónica Gago

Javier Milei, President of Argentina, became globally famous because of the chainsaw he hung around his head at campaign rallies, promising to make deep cuts to the state, and performing masculinist predatory capitalism. He won the election and took office in December 2023, just when Argentina was supposed to celebrate forty years of recovery of democracy. Milei's government is the radicalisation of Mauricio Macri's neoliberal government (2015-2019), which reached power following three terms of progressive governments led by Néstor Kirchner and Cristina Fernández de Kirchner (2003-2015). During Macri's government, a political and economic counter-offensive took shape, such that the height of feminist mobilisations for abortion rights coincided with the IMF's return to the country. Macri's electoral force was definitive in Milei's victory and the assembling of his government (Milei won without a political party and without a parliamentary majority). Macri's victory was the first time since the military dictatorship (1976-1983) that a president took office with an explicitly right-wing programme, and with a right organised as a political party, overcoming the schema of a 'military party'.

We must also consider the sequence that followed Macri's electoral defeat at the hands of a moderate progressive (Alberto Fernández, 2019-2023), spanning the first two years of the pandemic and the inflationary crisis of the second half of his term. Milei's government thus came to power in the midst of an economic crisis growing at the rate of a 200% annual increase in inflation. The political and subjective impact of hyper-inflation cannot be underestimated. This is one characteristic that is not present on such a scale in other countries in which the far right is on the rise. Material limits on expectations of how to live, consume and work are what is at stake in this unfolding of hyper-inflation. The economic frustration that Milei tapped into and addressed with his promises of stabilisation won him the election, but this does not form a stable base of legitimacy to the extent that the affectation of austerity advances.

In what follows I analyse the emergence of Milei's ultra-right government in terms of three ideas: 1) as a reactionary response to a sequence of struggles led by feminism and its way of politicising social reproduction; 2) as the effect of a subjectivity trained in an economic crisis that is financially 'resolved' with debt in order to live; and 3) as the symptom of a crisis of representation of the democratic political system expressed as the right-wing's attempt to capture radicalness. Finally, I suggest the notion of 'fascistisation of social reproduction' as a way to connect these ideas.

Human capital against social reproduction

The Ministry of Human Capital provides a synthetic image of the government of Javier Milei – the self-proclaimed first 'anarcho-capitalist' government in Argentina and the world. This new state institution absorbs the ministries of Labour, Education, Social Development, Health and Culture. It is headed by a graduate of Family Sciences from Opus Dei university, Sandra Pettovello, who presents herself as an 'expert in mindfulness, life crises and grief, relationships and couples'.[1] This sounds like one of Melinda Cooper's case studies for the marriage between neoliberalism and conservatism: an 'evolution' of the libertarian and paleo-conservative alliance that attempts to create compatibility between extreme market freedom, state deregulation and hierarchies of class, gender and race to guarantee the private sphere as a radically non-free sphere.[2] Among other cuts to public services, the new Minister has cut public support for *comedores populares*, community-run soup kitchens where ten million impoverished people obtain food today. The majority of these *comedores* arose directly from social struggles and movements of previous decades, and are especially maintained by women's community work.

The Minister has also persecuted those who receive social welfare benefits, with deliberately cruel attacks aimed at mothers who take their children to protests, and at these spaces' form of political organisation. Historically they have been closely tied to social movements, often directly established and managed by movements themselves, rather than charities or NGOS. These tasks of social reproduction, which have become social and communitarian because of the crisis, have to do with a politicisation of the subsidies coming from the state by social movements, whose history goes back to the 2001 Argentinian economic crisis. The political genealogy of the valorisation of reproductive labour, particularly in popular economies whose leadership is clearly feminised, is a key element in understanding ways of self-management (hundreds of worker-managed factories, self-managed food production and health care, and community organisation of security and neighbourhood infrastructure) in critical conditions (mass unemployment, impoverishment, inflation).[3] The feminist radicalisation of such infrastructures was due to the effect produced in them by the feminist massification in the streets over the last ten years, which enabled the challenging of gender mandates and affirming of feminist and queer leaderships in those territories and experiences.

The Minister has made an absolute shift: now privileging religious institutions and retrograde organisations, one of which is known for its president's statement that 'A woman must make an effort to offer man both her physical and her moral virginity'.[4] The Ministry of Human Capital thus functions to discipline and criminalise forms of politicised social reproduction in Argentina that had successfully disputed resources from the state through popular and feminist struggles during a crisis of formal waged work going back decades. This new Ministry condenses Milei's plan, who campaigned shouting 'Afuera!' ['Out!'], promising to do away with ministries, public budgets and social rights. This image (which became a viral video) fits perfectly with what Judith Butler calls a 'fascist passion for stripping rights'.[5] In this text I want to ask who this excites and why.

Meanwhile, in July, Milei created a new Ministry of Deregulation and Transformation of the State, whose Minister was involved in the financial crisis of 2001, supporting the banks, and in taking out the IMF loan during Mauricio Macri's government. This is yet another scene that demonstrates the reverberation of a 'neoliberalism in ruins', to use Wendy Brown's formulation that continues finding new meanings today;[6] but deploying its 'original violence' in a new moment. Speaking about the political situation in Argentina today means situating ourselves in the middle of an experiment that is, at the same time, both directly global and strongly local. However, both elements can become trivial: Milei becomes just another representative of the far-right constellations that are sprouting forth like mushrooms in the face of social discontent, and his particularities are understood as eccentricities, colourful data points, linked to a specific conjuncture in a 'Third World' country. I want to push beyond this schema to ask what is novel about the global nature of his wager, and how the local element of its roots are not limited to national specificities.

Plunder neoliberalism

Milei's electoral victory must be understood as catalysing rejection of the precarity that existed prior to, and was made worse by, the pandemic. To put it directly: popular frustration with precarity helped bring Milei to power, making visible a growing and polymorphous precariousness that seems to be marginalised again and again when political discourses focus on rights and inclusion policies. But his victory must also be understood as a challenge and reaction to the massiveness of grassroots feminist struggles in Argentina, which proposed responding to this precarity through non-individualistic and non-authoritarian formulas at the same time as they achieved political victories, such as legal, safe and free abortion.

I conceptualise Milei's government in terms of the practical rehearsal of a new type of neoliberalism that I call 'plunder neoliberalism'. By 'plunder neoliberalism' I am referring to the combination of (1) an extractivist acceleration of neoliberalism, which speeds up the territorial partition of the country by provinces according to their possession of resources (especially lithium) and, on the other hand, (2) governing by finance, which wages war on the population in its everyday life by infiltrating social reproduction with financial apparatuses such as debt (which was expanded in unimaginable ways during the pandemic through 'financial inclusion' policies), and now reaches limit-moments in the face of the acceleration of impoverishment through hyper-inflation.

Talking about 'plunder neoliberalism' is a way of theorising the strategic war against social reproduction as a contemporary form of counter-insurgency. We are now facing a different level of austerity politics – a level of extractivism, dispossession and plunder that can only take place in combination with the extreme criminalisation of social conflict and logics of war. In this sense, I want to propose understanding the terrain of social reproduction as one in which a 'fascism from below', as Zeynep Gambetti has argued, has taken root.[7] In the case of Argentina, I am referring to a particularly rapid and aggressive process through impoverishment due to inflation and in which a counter-revolution to feminist politicisation is deployed. In turn, I attempt to connect this process with what I earlier theorised as 'neoliberalism from below' to problematise a moment of neoliberalism in Latin America at a time when post-neoliberalism was being spoken of in regard to the rise of progressive governments.[8]

In that connection between neoliberalism and fascism from below, which is also a form of *mutation*,[9] I want to analyse the dispute over what is perceived as a crisis of social reproduction in order to develop the notion of the 'fascistisation of social reproduction', a notion that originally arose in conversation with Silvia Federici.[10] I want to specifically focus on the current moment as a renewal of counterinsurgency tactics related to an 'economy of obedience'. Here we can see that there is also a dispute over the diagnosis of different forms of violence, just when the massiveness of feminism managed to denaturalise violence in everyday life in ways 'that concretely changed the lives of our comrades', as a neighbourhood activist said in an assembly a few months ago. At the same time, this is a dispute over the militarisation of social conflict (by state and para-state forms) and the mobilisation of reactionary subjectivation (which the ultra right is taking advantage of today).

The government's whole package of laws and decrees points to a logic of a predatory capitalism, symbolised by the chainsaw Milei waves around his head at rallies as he promises to make cuts to the state. The velocity of this shock places us in the landscape of a *capitalist revolution* that uses social media to eliminate political mediations. It is for that reason that feminisms – involved with concrete struggles ranging from wages to pensions, from the Trans Employment Quota[11] to housing struggles – cause so much discomfort for those right-wingers who continue singling out feminist movements and thinking as a public enemy. Feminisms, in opposition, propose a formula of reclaiming and caring for the commons that questions privileges while simultaneously claiming rights, and continue to put the focus on social transformation at the same time as making specific demands.

We cannot automatically assume an immediate translation between the fascist mode of government and the motives of its voters. Instead, we must investigate the subjective pillars built by neoliberal dispossession to triumph at the ballot boxes and to interpellate youth sectors, especially men and the precarious. For a subjectivity that has already been trained over years of neoliberalism, austerity measures are a mandate to optimise and monetise one's own resources. In other words, it is the strategisation of our own impoverishment in favour of capital. But it is also a key element for understanding the project of 'patriarchal restoration', to quote Butler again, that it drives.[12] Rights are now experienced as 'privileges', as they are increasingly scarce and abstract under neoliberalism, leading to the individual, rather than collective, vindication of rights.

In previous work I coined the concept 'neoliberalism from below' to explain how neoliberalism takes root in subjectivities that, in order to progress, are forced to battle in harsh conditions marked by the dispossession of public infrastructure and, furthermore, to do so without capital. It is in that desire for popular prosperity, the desire to live better, where the strategic composition of micro-entrepreneurial elements with formulas of self-management takes place. This assembles an ability to negotiate and dispute state, neighbourhood and community resources with overlapping relationships of kinship, work and loyalty connected to the territory. At a time when post-neoliberal horizons were up for debate, in the midst of a wave of progressive and popular governments in Latin America, I was interested in delving into neoliberal subjective dynamics that unfolded in very different contexts from those imagined by Foucault.

The neoliberal dynamic is combined in a problematic and effective way with persevering vitalism (inflected as a desire for prosperity) that always clings to the expansion of freedoms, pleasure and affect. In my research at the time, focused on informalised and popular economies, this led me to trace how notions of freedom, calculation and obedience had changed in everyday life, projecting a new rationality and collective affectivity. I used Foucault to analyse the features of exploitation in informalised labour, not in terms of marginal and minority figures, but rather as mass dynamics. Perhaps here it is a matter of thinking Foucault against Foucault: if he argues that neoliberalism de-proletarianises the subject by making one an entrepreneur of oneself, I try to think about what kind of proletarian that is (as an entrepreneur). This perspective forces us to analyse antagonisms loaded with ambivalence, to untangle the permanent tension between immanence and strategy.

I made precise use of Foucault's work to understand governmentality in terms of the expansion of freedoms and therefore to analyse the types of productive and multiscalar assemblages involved in contemporary neoliberalism as a mode of government and production of reality, which also overflows that government. I argued that, in Latin America, Foucault must be extended by rooting the critique of neoliberalism as a mode of power, domination and dispossession in the experience of the revolts that took place at the beginning of the century; while also debating the images and forms of political happiness implicated in diverse notions of freedom, which simultaneously compete and cooperate under neoliberalism. Foucault must also be extended with a second element: neoliberalism in our region is immediately violent, from its origins. Authoritarianism is not *ex post* deviation. The 'original violence' of neoliberalism shows that neoliberalism emerged in response to revolutionary struggles. It must be understood, then, as a regime of social existence and a political mandate that was installed through state and para-state massacres of popular and armed insurgencies. It was consolidated through dictatorships which implemented deep structural reforms in the subsequent decades, following the logic of 'structural adjustment' policies around the globe. Friedrich Hayek's and Milton Friedman's visits to the region in those years, and their support for Pinochet's dictatorship, are a special chapter for developing the doctrinaire component that neoliberalism had in our countries. In other words, Latin America presents a deep archive for examining the relationship between neoliberalism and fascism.

At the time I was interested in understanding how the challenge to neoliberalism's political legitimacy was combined with the recognition of a political and productive subjectivity that assimilated self-management and social programmes achieved through struggle. In turn, that antagonism against austerity was also incorporated as a measurable value: as a capacity of management, effort and will to progress and, therefore, *indebtable*. The flows of debt for a precarious and politically organised population built a sort of irrigation delta from below that responded first to a moment of a consumer boom and later to periods of austerity under Mauricio Macri's government (2015-2019). This connection between financialisation 'from below' and the making of a political subjectivity of entrepreneurship among dispossessed sectors was also important for understanding the first series of electoral defeats of progressive governments that, although not much acknowledged at the time, is part of the more or less generalised consensus today.

However, we now find ourselves in a third moment. Previously, I analysed the financialisation of popular economies, of economies of reproduction that expanded into territories and were not only confined to homes, as a way of detecting the role that finance plays under neoliberalism to guarantee social reproduction in a private way. In turn, there were two moments of its functioning. First, in relation to a debt that was part of a consumer boom associated with a commodity boom in the country and, *at the same time*, strongly associated with social movements' anti-austerity demands. Second, debt was channeled into basic goods of food, medicine and housing payments when the country returned to the IMF (2018) at the same time as feminist politicisation was deployed on the mass level. Now we are facing a third moment in which the mandate for austerity has managed to inoculate itself in the population, to the point that Milei's phrases such as 'there is no money' have been taken up as part of popular language. Then, the question is: What is the role of that financialisation in a situation of economic war declared against social reproduction? How does the financialisation of social reproduction provide concrete situations for the acceleration of fascistisation of that terrain of struggle?

The politics of cruelty

Milei simultaneously vindicates the military dictatorship of the 1970s and 1980s and the Washington Consensus of the 1990s, but under the 'programmatic' form of a troll. He is proud of drawing his power directly from capital: it is the great owners who transfer their aura to him. Milei's government proposes a synthesis in a repudiation of democratic forms, drawing from a generalised feeling of their restrictive, classist and racist character. It is a clear attempt to colonise the frustration with democracy. In that register, Milei calls forth a population that has been trained in a financial subjectivation 'from below' to confront precarity, that is intimately aware of the limits of state intervention to produce equality. It is this subjectivation that advances and renders legible a certain notion of freedom and the proposal of forms of property that are paradoxically affirmed in contexts of dispossession.

One of the features of Milei's governance that stands out is the velocity of the ultra-neoliberal reforms that are already being implemented. During his campaign, he promised even greater austerity measures than those demanded by the IMF, and that is exactly what he has been doing. Milei wants to star in this capitalist revolution because it is located in a geopolitical moment in which he wagers on complicity with Elon Musk (whose erotic-entrepreneurial celebration of Milei's speech at Davos in 2024, shared on X, is not only explicitly disturbing, but also forces us to analyse and combat its efficacy), Trump and Netanyahu.

At the Davos Economic Forum, Milei – in his first time on the global stage after his election – singled out radical feminism and environmentalism as the main public enemies. Thus he positioned both movements as synonymous with social justice, the so-called 'aberration' that he aims to eradicate. It is necessary to analyse that association and, to do so, explain that the feminist struggle in our country is also a struggle against extractivism: that is, against the plundering of common goods and, especially, financial speculation over land which directly transfers onto food prices. In that sense, the feminist movement in Argentina has proposed social reproduction as a battlefield that is currently traversed by hunger and plunder.

A 'pedagogy of cruelty' is added to this shock. The Argentine anthropologist Rita Segato has elaborated on the concept to speak of gender-based violence and sexist aggression as a form of the pact of masculinity, which became visible at the beginning of the Ni Una Menos movement around 2015.[13] Today this term goes beyond the vocabulary of feminisms and names the type of verbal, political, economic and symbolic violence exercised by this government that is practiced daily on social media. It brings together forms of insult and mistreatment, celebrating lay-offs and memes that banalise paedophilia at the same time as comprehensive sexual education programmes are decimated.

In the book *History of Argentinian Cruelty: Julio A. Roca and the Genocide of Native Populations*, Osvaldo Bayer defines racism using the term 'cruelty' to describe the torture of the Indigenous population in the nineteenth century.[14] Yet, he also associates it with a social form:

> Cruelty rose to the surface in a Creole Europeanized, profoundly racist, society. The thinker Juan Bautista Alberdi, one of the fathers of the National Constitution [and one of Milei's reference points], wrote 'I do not know any distinguished people of our societies with Pehuenche or Araucano surnames. Does anyone know a gentleman who is proud of being an Indian? Would any of us let our sister or daughter marry an Indian from Araucanía? I would prefer an English shoemaker a thousand times over'.

Here there is a key 'genealogy' of cruelty: directly linked to the foundational racism of the nation-state and the descriptions of extermination that Bayer historicises. But it is also, as Alberdi says in the quote, linked to blood lineages: extermination always takes place in favour of certain surnames and families in which land and racist pride are concentrated.

This foundational association between the nation-state and cruelty is what Jacques Derrida, in his keynote address to the 'General States of Psychoanalysis', emphasises as he connects cruelty with sovereignty:[15]

> If the drive for power or the cruelty drive is irreducible, older, more ancient than the principles (the pleasure principle or the reality principle, which are basically the same, the same in *differance*, I would like to say), then no politics will be able to eradicate it. Politics can only domesticate it, differ and defer it, learn to negotiate, compromise indirectly but without illusion with it, and it is this indirection, this differing/deferring detour, this system of

differantial relays and delays that will dictate Freud's at once optimistic and pessimistic politics, which are courageously disabused, resolutely sobered up.[16]

Photo by Michael Runyan

When I speak of the politics of cruelty to characterise Milei's government, I am referring to the way in which institutional politics deliberately, and with joy, abandons any mechanism of negotiation and postponement with respect to violence. It is in this way that cruelty appears or, better, reappears. A paradox thus emerges: the politics of cruelty would mark the end of political mediations aimed at keeping it at a distance. However, in doing so, it produces politics. The politics of cruelty wagers on governing without governing (if we understand governing as the art of mediations that dissimulate and metabolise violence). The politics of cruelty relies on direct, spectacularised violence as a mechanism that produces *desensitisation*.

It is worth repeating that this is not new. It is repeated, it occurs, in certain moments: the issue is to understand the logic of that repetition. When does cruelty emerge as an undisguisable element of the phenomenology of violence? In moments in which politics is pure conquest. The ultra-right, as several analyses have already stated, capitalises on and encourages this drive of cruelty, which is also an affect of self-salvation in the face of generalised precarity and insecurity. How can we understand the spread of Milei's campaign slogan that 'there is no money' for justifying the 'sacrifice' of the waiting sustained during these months? That temporality of waiting combines austerity and personal debt, creating a speculative 'bubble' at the subjective level that, however, has limits. Cruelty become politics exhibits a joy associated with the exercise of direct violence; it practices a spectacular reiteration that seeks to desensitise and deploy a historical affiliation. Those three elements – pleasure, desensitisation, history – must be analysed at the level of the government but also in terms of its activations and implications at the social level.

This brings us to one of Milei's particular qualities as an ultra-right leader: he is not a traditional nationalist. Milei is a member of the financial sector with close connections to investment funds and a defender of the global institutionality of concentrated capital and imperial powers. Milei celebrates the holders of capital as heroes after promoting money laundering, capital flight and tax evasion. He represents an extreme right-wing in a situation of extreme 'internal colonialism'. Milei also goes beyond Bolsonaro because of the genocide in Gaza and his alignment with the United States and Israel that create another scenario for him. But this is also because Milei does not play at nationalism, as Trump does. In Milei, the direct colonial dimension of his subjugation, his power and his effectiveness emerges. His position is that of an extreme 'internal colonialism' – to quote the Mexican sociologist Pablo González Casanova[17] – where it becomes necessary to deploy an 'internal war' to assert the positions of colonial subordination. With that I want to emphasise that the process of breaking the country's territorial unity, linked to a proposal of extractive businesses and tax benefits, is directly connected to colonial subordination at the global level and crossing thresholds of internal violence. The government has already announced the targeted militarisation of 'resource' zones.

Modalities of debt

Milei enacts a government without masses in the street: It is clear that Milei's fascism – unlike other historical fascisms – does not have the capacity to win the street; it wagers on reaching a mass level online in social and addictive media (a characteristic already pointed out by Enzo Traverso in thinking about the virtual masses of contemporary fascism[18]). Milei won with the proposal to radicalise forms of financial governance – in which everyone who has to deal with precarity is forced to engage in speculation – combined with a reactionary, misogynist and patriarchal discourse.

There are two key characteristics of the novelty of the neoliberal shock that we are experiencing: the velocity and intensity of the violence that it takes on as a mode of government. This is because Milei extracts his power directly from the corporations with the most concentrated capital, in a moment of the accelerated reconfiguration of capitalism towards an extractive and war model. He does not bank on a logic of governmentality, but rather one of pure destruction. However, that destruction seems to be 'contained' by precarity itself. What are its limits?

Finance incorporated into the management of precarity has built a capillary network capable of providing private and extremely expensive financing to resolve the problems of everyday life that arise from austerity and inflation. In 2018, when Mauricio Macri's government took out an unprecedented amount of debt from the IMF, that indebtedness accelerated and intensified. As Luci Cavallero and I showed in the book *A Feminist Reading of Debt*, since then the destinations and uses of debt have decisively turned to paying for food and medicine, and, during the pandemic, rent.[19] Finance, through (increasingly diversified) debt, has made it possible to avoid – or at least has slowed down – the situation of *scarcity* that was seen in other moments of crisis (the 2001 crisis, for example).

How did this transcendence of scarcity via consumer debt nevertheless lead to a situation where so many people have internalised the government message that we are living beyond our means? Only by understanding the moral force with which inflation is invested (a sort of punishment by the 'forces of heaven', according to the presidential rhetoric), is it possible to understand how its lack of control becomes the ultimate scene of sacrifice and purification. This is a key point argued by Milei's 'inflationary crusade'. This allows for undoing his promises to put an end to inflation and point to dollarisation as the ultimate project.

Debt articulated with an entrepreneurial drive (a condition that is completely compatible with work subsidised by the state) is what allows platform workers (from virtual market sellers to delivery workers), for example, to buy their means of production (of communication and transportation). It is a paradoxical inverted situation: workers *must be owners* of the means with which they produce. Of course, we are talking about cheap means especially used in the service sector or in spaces of informal sales or cooperatives. Even so, it is a modality that expands throughout the most impoverished sectors, that has increased due to working at home during the pandemic, and that also reaches middle-class sectors (for example, loans to teachers to buy computers and to be able to work from a home office). The acquisition of these means of production takes place through debt: once again, radical dispossession is contained under a schema of property ownership (I am going to be the 'owner' of what I am buying).

Understanding how debt extracts value from household economies, non-waged economies, from economies historically considered to be non-productive, allows for seeing financial apparatuses as true mechanisms of value extraction and the moralisation of existences unleashed by the gender mandate (that is, of a certain articulation between reproduction and production). Thus it is a matter of analysing the physiognomy of what is traditionally called the labour conflict beyond its usual coordinates (a waged, union, masculine framework) to think about how the financial system is, on the one hand, a response to a specific sequence of struggles and, on the other hand, a dynamic of containment that organises a certain experience of the current crisis.

This cycle of debt responds to the recent sequence of feminist struggles and to a financial reading about certain modes of existence. The feminist movement politicises the crisis of social reproduction in a new and radical way as a crisis that is both civilisational and a crisis of the patriarchal structure of society. It is a movement that is anti-neoliberal in concrete ways and that operates in a class-based articulation with popular economy workers and unions; it is anti-colonial, seeking articulation with those who are leading anti-extractive conflicts (from peasant movements to environmental assemblies).

Feminism has shifted the lens of productive spatialities and, as Federici argues, allows for counting the full duration of the working day, including what takes place in kitchens and bedrooms, neighbourhoods and community spaces. It is that fabric of laborious spatiality where the work of reproducing life takes place, and in which work is carried out, that mixes self-management with scarce public resources, carrying out social tasks that complete and/or replace deficient or non-existent services, at the same time as they sustain a labour force subjected to ever more precarity. A focus on variation and difference in geographies of social reproduction allows for recognising the historical and geographical construction of the reproduction-production binary and that a dependency on waged labour outside the household has only ever been the norm in certain times and places. Centring agricultural work, work in the community or work in the 'popular economies' thus substantially alters our understanding of the geographies of both social reproduction and production.

But then the pandemic came: tensions around freedom and care intensified. It also radicalised the right-wing's critique of state 'intervention' in the media and on the street, capturing a critique of institutions of confinement, which police and punish. From our analysis at the time, I highlighted what was tied together around the category of 'essential work'. Essential work condenses a strong paradox: it names a re-naturalisation of those tasks and their association with certain bodies, now applauded for their work but not sufficiently remunerated. This produces a particular twist: it is spoken of as work but, upon classifying it as essential, it seems to cease to be so. Its value is recognised but it seems to be fundamentally symbolic and emergency-based. We see this practiced on a large scale on those tasks and many jobs connected to social reproduction: it is the same as the historical manoeuvre of naturalisation of the work of reproduction, only now out in the open and no longer in the enclosure of the household sphere. Meanwhile, at the same time, there is a 'return' to the home under the mode of expanding telework, reproductive tasks and new care responsibilities.

While one reading of essential work could be that it seeks to legitimise the gratuity and/or insufficient remuneration of certain tasks carried out in domestic territories, we can also identify the inscription of accumulated struggles there. Would it have been possible to explicitly connect essentialness with reproductive tasks without the prior politicisation of care that feminisms have put on the agenda at the mass level in recent years? At the time of the rise of feminist politicisation, the pandemic functioned as a handbrake and, at the same time, a moment of over-exploitation. This led to greater indebtedness. But it also led to a recombination of notions of freedom and obedience: here I mean the ambivalence of more debt as a device to produce more possibilities of doing things, but this freedom always entangled and combined with the discipline of debt. Thinking about that displacement which constructs the centrality of household debt also implies understanding the forces that debt manages to command as an organiser of increasingly precarious work, including illegal economies.

A crucial dimension in relation to the study of household indebtedness is understanding its relation with, largely feminised, unpaid work. This is a methodological key that our feminist perspective on debt adds, one that was fundamental for understanding the pandemic's impact on domestic spatiality (and 'the sexual division of debt', to use Isabelle Guerin's term.[20]) It is also fundamental to underscore and qualify the relation between debt and labour, because it demonstrates that debt cannot be delinked from its dependence on labour and land.

The fascistisation of social reproduction

A whole variation of the concept of social reproduction opens up when we comprehend it from the present. This is also due to a fundamental feature of contemporary neoliberalism: the deepening of the crisis of social reproduction that it produces is cushioned by an increase in feminised labour, unpaid and subjected to the blackmail of family and individual responsibilisation. The privatisation of public services, or the restriction of their scope, means that those tasks (health care, feeding, childcare and so on) must be supplied by women, lesbians, travestis, and trans persons as unpaid or badly paid and obligatory work. I believe it is nevertheless insufficient to speak of a crisis of social reproduction. Rather, this crisis is the beginning of a sequence: the crisis is followed by a war against social reproduction, which seeks to lay the foundations for its fascistisation. This implies, first, that we need to understand that the crisis of social reproduction produced by neoliberal policies is answered by a politicisation of social reproduction. It is this feminist politicisation which is attacked in the form of a war against social reproduction. The rise of the ultra-right must be explained in relation to these dynamics and to the search for the intensification of plunder and the familiarist, racist and biologicist keys to provoke the fascistisation of social reproduction.

In the heat of the massification of feminism, in popular and feminised economies on our continent, social reproduction exceeds the limits of the household, to refer to networks and communities, to be able to be understood as the articulation of forms of doing, of obtaining incomes, of disputing recognition, organising the supply of essential services and challenging the hetero cis family framework. I refer to the proliferation of communal and neighbourhood bonds, of organisational forms and cooperatives that assemble, in changing ways, with the dynamics of struggle, but also with popular entrepreneurship and initiatives that create infrastructure or maintain certain ancestral practices in new contexts.

My thesis here is that the politicisation of the crisis of social reproduction maps the lines of conflict that inhabit a neoliberal subjectivation in contexts of dispossession *and* it rejects the conservative-familial forms of containing this privatisation. For this reason, it allows for a reading of the totality in an anti-capitalist key and provides an internationalist dimension to specific, rooted, local struggles. This seems to me to be a key point, also taking into account the fact that the struggles which highlight the question of social reproduction as antagonism with capital directly intervene in international politics today: we can think about struggles around abortion or pensions. These struggles have an impact on the global level, proving that the reproductive terrain is decisive in battles over political subjectivity that articulate neoliberalism and extreme conservatism.

Social reproduction – which includes social relations as well as public policies, forms of relations as collective equipment and habits – is organised according to the dynamics of social struggle both in its historical content and specific modalities, therefore it is a decisive battleground due to the way in which capitalist contradictions can be radicalised. Furthermore, unlike other analyses, it is impossible for social reproduction to be divided, separated from the strategic plane of the plane of subjectivities in struggle. It is also this feminist, queer, migrant and popular politicisation of social reproduction that allows for reading a dynamic of neoliberalism that no longer only adjusts to the logics of entrepreneurship of the self and its subjective modulation in adaptive terms, but rather new tendencies of direct violence, formulating logics of war in specific territories. And it is the feminist movement that has been denouncing these new logics of war and 'regimes of war'.[21]

Social reproduction has long been discussed as a way of defining interdependence in a materialist way. These two arguments are key for a feminist epistemology that looks at production *from below*. It is also *from below* that we analyse the proliferation of neoliberalism and fascism. The concrete terrain of their entrenchment is the material mutations in social reproduction. The category of *war*, already used by feminisms to account for new coordinates of violence, becomes more strategic than ever.[22] The war against the conditions of reproduction of the population, and the war against the conditions of reproduction of struggles, are articulated with war as the global stage, to which the ultra-right can appeal to polarise local scenarios when social protest is on the rise. Militarisation is the highest stage of financial warfare.

The dispute over what is perceived as a crisis at the level of social reproduction is important in order to develop the notion of 'fascistisation of social reproduction'.[23] I use this term to refer to a political form that allows for the power of capital to advance through reducing investment in social reproduction *against* its feminist, queer, migrant and popular politicisation while intensifying the impulse toward violent ways of managing reproduction through 'financial violence' and targeting women, the LGBTQ and migrant population as a contemporary form of war.

Inflation is an accelerator of the crisis as a strategy of the fascistisation of social reproduction. It points to women and feminists responsible for social reproduction as the opposite of 'human capital' and causes antifeminism to grow as a vector of reactionary politicisation. But we can also see it concretely in the way that an ultraneoliberal labour reform – always in the name of 'modernisation' – was negotiated in Argentina in the first six months of Milei's government: to try to win its approval in Congress, two issues that they want to negotiate with unions are put forth as bargaining chips: pensions for housewives and parental leave *and* the complete deregulation of the few safeguards in place for informalised economies (such as the simplified tax scheme for informal workers, ways of demonstrating relations of dependency and so on).[24] Once again, rights related to the social reproduction of feminised and informalised sectors are put up as leverage to maintain the borders of 'waged work'. That simultaneity demonstrates the revolutionary character of feminist practices located in territories subjected to dispossession and financialisation.

If Milei turns the whole country into a 'sacrifice zone', to use a term deployed under neo-extractivism to delimit the areas that are offered to business and that 'pay the price' with their contamination and environmental degradation, it is because business does not allow for any dissimulation. What was a 'zone' with borders, becomes a generalised project, without borders or limits. In Argentina, federalism itself is up for debate and Milei's allies are defending the so-called 'Desert Campaign' – the nineteenth-century genocide of Indigenous populations to steal their land. This is not simply an anachronism in a time of the rise of finance. On the contrary, it demonstrates the capacity of neo-extractivism, when plunder becomes a political logic, to reorganise both the 'national' space and political temporality, producing a fold between the nineteenth and twenty-first century.

The abyss of financialisation

The acceleration of economic violence through financial extractivism finds in the platforms its favourite means. Since the pandemic, the so-called 'FinTech' (financial technology) companies have consolidated and expanded as means of payment and, above all, as sources of indebtedness.[25] It is no longer the state with banks, but rather *fintech* which produces an experience of speculation that is immanent to survival.

These questions are key for understanding the political management of the 'patience' of those subjected to austerity, the momentary effectiveness over popular subjectivity of phrases such as 'there is no money' or 'we have to make sacrifices', which attempt to make the language of austerity into a language of the masses.

On the one hand, public spending austerity and plunder of public infrastructure is channelled into increasing private indebtedness. On the other hand, the psychic logic behind the acceptance of the idea that 'the government has no money' functions as part of a logic of sacrifice: we are guilty of hyper-inflation because it is part of public spending profligacy. The entrepreneurship subjectivity fuelled by 'neoliberalism from below' is interpellated as part of the 'solution' at the same time that it relates to the most affected population. I am interested in thinking about the logic of austerity as it imposes itself as a logic of veridiction, to use a Foucauldian term. It reveals something of the truth of scarcity that debt conceals. The contradictory logic is evident: it is that very austerity that forces us to take on more debt.

Along this line, social protest provides us with the coordinates for understanding how debt has organised its expansion as an apparatus of government. The feminist reading of debt, which connects the exploitation of reproductive labour to modes of territorial governmentality (and thus exposes the dependence on debt in respect to work and land), practices this manoeuvre: it questions the channelling of financial obligation into household debt particularly targeting women and female heads of household at a time when the feminist movement expresses its massive force in the streets *and* in homes; and it denounces a diverse range of extractive dynamics, inquiring into their connections. But later, referring to a third moment, debt to fund social reproduction seems to be reaching a limit due to the velocity and cruelty of impoverishment.

Here a greater problem emerges that can be considered an open question, which has especially been raised by feminist movements: what are the political tools of protest and negotiation of a labour force that lies in the intersection between financial (and platform) capitalism and non-guaranteed social reproduction? In the press release for the eighth review of the Extended Facility arrangement in May 2024, the IMF says that the government met the goals 'with margins'. What is this over-achievement if not the deployment of an economic war against the population's survival? The death drive gives way to finance. Milei has said that 'if people were not making ends meet, they would be dead'. Never mind the fact that people are literally dying due to the lack of medication and the lesbophobic cruelty promoted by the government, this is the scene in which debt 'offers' solutions to avoid dying of hunger. Marcos Galperín, the most successful platform capitalist in Argentina, does business thanks to the financial mediation of scarce resources from social programmes, while forcing their beneficiaries to go into debt through his platform, to attempt small 'speculations' to pay for dollarised food. But it also absorbs and exploits unpaid financial labour that consists of surviving income poverty through small-scale financial carry operations that consume time and, more than anything, one's mental health.

I want to emphasise this third moment of indebtedness that operates in an extreme scenario: in the midst of an all-out war against the social reproduction of the majorities in order to produce its fascistisation. Here what is at stake is the limit and the abyss of the financialisation of social reproduction, its productivity at the level of political subjectivities, and, ultimately, thresholds of social violence. It is on that same terrain where the 'fascistisation' of social reproduction is both activated and becomes abysmal. The dimension of 'patriarchal restoration' that it takes on is key for understanding how it seeks to annul other reproductive forms, those supported by other relationships and experiences and politicisation. If the notion of war on the plane of social reproduction is based on the idea of an antagonism between social reproduction and capital,[26] the intervention of feminist politicisation has exacerbated this antagonism in recent years. We know that social reproduction is itself a necessary component of the reproduction of capital. How does feminist, queer, migrant and popular politicisation modify and subvert it?

Without a doubt, we can argue that feminist politicisation *divided* the social reproduction of capital in such a way as to make its antagonism visible, and Milei and his Ministry of Human Capital are attempting violent recomposition. Does the current war imply a project of capitalist reconstruction of social reproduction? Here I have attempted to take the notion of the fascistisation of social reproduction in that direction, where the logic of a neoliberalism of plunder seeks to attack, restore and recompose the reproduction of capital. Under this sequence, the finance/debt nexus is a fundamental element, increasingly 'demanded' in its cycles of expropriation, of plunder.

Translated by Liz Mason Deese

Verónica Gago is a feminist researcher at the National Scientific and Technological Research Council of Argentina and teaches political science and gender theory at the University of Buenos Aires and the Universidad Nacional de San Martín. She is the author of Feminist International *(Verso 2020), and is now at the Chaire Internationale de Philosophie Contemporaine de l'Université Paris 8.*

Notes

1. Roxama Spanda, 'Sandra Pettovello: The super minister in charge of Education, Health, Labor, and Social Development', *Pagina 12*, 24 November 2023, https://www.pagina12.com.ar/688481-la-superministra

2. Melinda Cooper, 'The Alt-Right: Neoliberalism, Libertarianism and the Fascist Temptation', *Theory, Culture & Society* 38:6 (2021).

3. For a more detailed genealogy of these political infrastructures of social reproduction, see Verónica Gago, *Feminist International: How to Change Everything* (London and New York: Verso, 2020), 125–30.

4. *Pagina 12*, 'The story of Abel Albino, the obscurantist pediatrician who is gaining ground in the Rosada Palace', 9 April 2024, https://www.pagina12.com.ar/710401-un-pediatra-ocurantista-vuelve-a-la-rosada

5. Judith Butler, *Who's Afraid of Gender?* (New York: Farrar, Straus and Giroux, 2024).

6. Wendy Brown, *In the Ruins of Neoliberalism: The Rise of Antidemocratic Politics in the West* (New York: Columbia University Press, 2019).

7. Zeynep Gambetti, 'Exploratory Notes on the Origins of New Fascisms', *Critical Times* 3:1 (2020).

8. Verónica Gago, *Neoliberalism From Below. Baroque Economies and Popular Pragmatics*, trans. Liz Mason Deese (London and New York: Verso, 2017).

9. William Callison and Zachary Manfredi, eds, *Mutant Neoliberalism: Market Rule and Political Rupture* (New York: Fordham University Press, 2020).

10. Silvia Federici and Verónica Gago, 'The revolution is now', *Ojalá*, https://www.ojala.mx/en/ojala-en/silvia-federici-the-revolution-is-now

11. Malen Denis, 'Argentina passed a quota for employing transgender people. It could save lives, advocates say', *The Washington Post*, 2 July 2021, https://www.washingtonpost.com/gender-identity/argentina-passed-a-quota-for-employing-transgender-people-it-could-save-lives-advocates-say/

12. Butler, *Who's Afraid?*

13. Rita Segato, "La pedagogía de la crueldad', *Pagina 12*, 29 May 2015, https://www.pagina12.com.ar/diario/suplementos/las12/13-9737-2015-05-29.html; and Rita Segato, *Contra-pedagogías de la crueldad* (Buenos Aires: Prometeo Libros, 2018).

14. Osvaldo Bayer, *Historia de la crueldad argentina. Julio A. Roca y el genocidio de los Pueblos Originarios* (Buenos Aires: Red de Investigadores en Genocidio y Política Indígena en Argentina, 2010).

15. Jacques Derrida, *Without Alibi*, trans. Peggy Kamuf (Stanford: Stanford University Press, 2002).

16. Derrida, *Without Alibi*, 252.

17. Pablo González Casanova, *Sobre el colonialismo interno* (Buenos Aires: Clacso, 2006).

18. Enzo Traverso, 'El fascismo como concepto transhistórico', *Herramienta*, 15 April 2024, https://www.herramienta.com.ar/el-fascismo-como-concepto-transhistorico

19. Luci Cavallero and Verónica Gago, *A Feminist Reading of Debt* (London: Pluto Press, 2021).

20. Isabelle Guérin, Santosh Kumar and G. Venkatasubramanian, *The Indebted Woman. Kinship, Sexuality, and Capitalism.* (Stanford University Press 2023).

21. Michael Hardt and Sandro Mezzadra, 'A global war regime', *New Left Review* 9.5 (2024), https://newleftreview.org/sidecar/posts/a-global-war-regime

22. For more on this, see Verónica Gago, 'Is politics possible today?', *Crisis and Critique* 9:2 (2022).

23. Federici, 'The revolution is now'.

24. Finally, the reform was approved, not even with the bargaining power of the unions willing to do so in order to preserve some of their sources of income. As analysed by the Asociación de Abogados y Abogadas Laboralistas, it legalises forms of labour fraud consisting of measures 'to hide a labour dependency relationship', extends the testing period indefinitely, incorporates striking as a cause for dismissal and the annulment of the aggravating circumstance of dismissal due to 'discrimination', among other regressive issues.

25. Luci Cavallero, Verónica Gago and Liz Mason-Deese, *The Home as Laboratory: Finance, Housing, and Feminist Struggle* (New York: Common Notions, 2024).

26. In a stronger sense than the contradictions raised by Nancy Fraser in 'Contradictions of Capital and Care', *New Left Review* 100 (2016). For an elaboration of this idea of the hidden antagonism of care, see Marta Malo, *La revuelta de los cuidados* (forthcoming) (Madrid: Suburbia, 2025).

Temporary autonomous friend

On Miesseroff's *Fag Hag* and Fox and Lane-McKinley's *fag/hag*

Sophie Lewis

'You don't have to be a couple to participate in the couple form', observed the writer and artist Hannah Black in an article published in *The New Inquiry* before the global onset of this coronavirus pandemic. We are participating when we presume others' romantic dyads, when we conceptualise uncoupled lives as 'single', and when we idealise marriage (not just when we marry or couple up). At the same time, as Black had already noted elsewhere, 'correct' embodiment of the couple form under capitalism is the exclusive purview of the structurally white, procreative nuclear household; 'for the rest of us – people of color, queers, queers of color, single women, and so on, that whole mixed and conflicted bag of lives – there is whatever we can make do with.' Classically, one such human accommodation to the probably-universal need for closeness and mutual recognition is the model of the pair comprising one non-lesbian woman and one queer man. Like many of my female friends, in adolescence, I was a bisexual 'hag' to many a 'fag': above all, to my semi-closeted brother – and closest friend – but also to a succession of more public best friends no one was ever going to mistake for my boyfriend. Fag/hag is a 'wrong form', as the writer Max Fox suggests, but sometimes we find in it a tolerable 'mode of moving through a wrong world.'

Two slim books about moving fag-and-hag-wise through the world have lately appeared in English, bearing more or less the same title, albeit rooted in engagement with different decades: respectively, the glorious late sixties and seventies, and the 'very rotten long nineties'.* The first of these, *Fag Hag* from PM Press, is a memoir by the Franco-Russian soixante-huitarde and veteran of the Front Homosexuel D'Action Révolutionnaire, Lola Miesseroff (*Fille à pédés* in the original), translated by Donald Nicholson-Smith. The second is the volume of epistolary family-abolitionist theorising *fag/hag*, published by the Australian collective Rosa Press, and authored by Fox together with another millennial native of the American west coast, Madeline Lane-McKinley. In an exchange of letters beginning amid the first COVID-19 pandemic lockdowns in 2020, Max and Madeline are empowered by their own longstanding communist-feminist comradeship and friendship to grapple with problems of solidarity across difference, as well as bittersweet legacies of utopian struggle waged by their forebears. One of these is Guy Hocquenghem, a former comrade of Miesseroff's, whose writing Fox has also translated. On a different, because reciprocal, plane of intimacy, throughout *fag/hag*, the two authors are united in a shared intensity of posthumous fagdom or hagdom vis-à-vis another gay Marxist – Christopher Chitty – who took his life in 2015, leaving behind life-changingly brilliant manuscripts for his surviving friends and lovers to adopt and nurture. If the goal of the FHAR, for Miesseroff, was '*explosons les codes sexuels!*' (let's explode sexual codification!), then the promiscuous bond between Max-Madeline-and-Chris – by turns co-parental, romantic, quasi-filial, comradely and sororal – does something similar to the received scripts for fag-hag relationships.

---

* Lola Miesseroff, *Fag Hag*, trans. Donald Nicholson-Smith (Oakland: PM Press, 2023) 144pp., £16.99 pb., 979 8 88744 010 1; Max Fox and Madeline Lane-McKinley, *fag/hag* (Sydney: Rosa Press, 2024), 100pp., $22.00 pb., 978 0 64523 922 5

In the received version, the spinster and the gay bachelor (closeted or not) form an alliance somewhere at the intersection of couple, kin and friends, united not by sexual intimacy but by disidentification from patriarchal heterosexuality. Gay community slang commonly ascribes centrality more to *her* than to *him* in this equation, as in 'queen bee', 'fairy princess', or 'Goldilocks' (get it? – and the bears). However, in mainstream English, the linguistic centre of gravity tends to be the *homo* element, as in 'beard' or 'fruit fly', where the woman represents the instrumentalised accessory or orbital, doubly abject because tarred with queerness, but only by association. Indeed, the sniffy assumption of many commentators has been that some kind of arrested development is in play: fag hags, Barbara Ellen wrote in a 2001 *Observer* article, 'borrow the gay sexual identity because they have little of their own.' Few people talk of hag fags, still less dyke bros. If a contest exists as to which half of the two, hag or fag, society has disparaged *more* as a figure of tragicomic thwartedness, immaturity or delusional ersatz coupledom, it doubtless remains moot. The main thing, to quote the French ACT UP veteran Hélène Hazéra, is that 'fag hags come in all shapes and sizes', reactionary and radical. Some such women undeniably belong to the Right, but many others, on the Left, 'cock a snook at gay male chauvinists and share their lives and loves with homosexual men' ever since (at least) the days of Charles Fourier and his early eighteenth-century 'new world of love'.

That said, who actually uses 'fag hag' in English today? Thirty-five years ago, the titan of queer theory Eve K. Sedgwick suggested that the 'ugly disyllabic' was as unreclaimable as the mid-century phrase 'n****r-lover'. Her remark was hyperbolic, but parallels existed between the Jim Crow-era vocabulary deployed to humiliate and de-gender white women for shirking their role in racial capitalist 'right' reproduction by sleeping with black men, and the AIDS-era one used to denigrate non-seropositive women who stood against the same regime of 'family values' in solidarity with a different (overlapping) population, also feared for its dysgenic contamination risk. Certainly in the years that followed Sedgwick's provocation, the consensus grew that the trope is misogynist and homophobic. A counter-current of ambivalent reclaimers accordingly emerged, such as the feminist scholar Cathy Crimmins, who self-designated thus even as she acknowledged: 'the fag-hag is the absolute bottom in a very complex emotional relationship' and 'a major symbol of unrequited love and failed femininity.' If hags are meant to be doomed by love for men who cannot return their feelings in kind, some women apparently want to narrate their unfulfillment that way, 'owning' the pathos of that imagined bottom rung.

In 2009, a much-shared *Salon* piece – 'Ladies, I'm Not Your Gay Boyfriend' – sought to put an end to reclamations, nihilist or otherwise. Thomas Rogers, the author, railed against the affluent women who arrogantly appropriate and condescendingly desexualise gays. Most of the 'overeager self-described "fag hags"' in the post-*Will and Grace* West were nothing like the brassy, culturally queer man-eating broads who originally defined it, *à la* Mae West or Liza Minnelli, Rogers said. In fact, they had 'square-jawed boyfriends' and 'seemingly little understanding of gay culture'. But crucially, even the 'fabulous gay-loving straight women of yore', were no longer make-or-break in the average gay's coming-of-age in many decreasingly homophobic regions of the world. Rogers concluded with a pointed, dignified hope that tomorrow's hags would call themselves 'something more accurate. Like "friend".' The disyllabic remains kicking nonetheless, possibly because the politics of friendship between men and women, and between male gays and feminists more specifically, has continued to generate considerable anxiety – as evidenced by neo-separatist discourses like the originally Korean boycott of men, '4B', the increased discussion of gay male misogyny, and the rise of transphobia in some 'LGB' circles.

Fag/hag is a thing it 'feels a bit too archaic to invoke', proposes Fox, 'but its persistence in my life at least means it needs theorizing.' The formula's undead persistence in culture is striking: the writer Grace Byron began 2025 with a celebratory essay, 'The f*g h*g grows up', in *Dirt magazine,* where she proclaimed: 'the FH has gotten sexier over the years.' Listicles still float about like the *LARB*'s 'Top 10 Fag Hags of Henry James: A Definitive Ranking', and *FAGHAG* is the title of Dylan Mulvaney's Edinburgh Fringe debut of 2024, which charts Mulvaney's gender transition, from twink into twink-loving woman, or hag. While New York's Miss Fag Hag Pageant has long since been retired, and the organisation SWISH (Straight Women in Support of Homos) rebranded itself, many veteran AIDS activists – such as the scholar of 'friend grief' Victoria Noe, author of *Fag Hags, Divas and Moms: The Legacy of Straight Women in the AIDS Community* – gamely defend the use of 'fag hag' to this day.

Miesseroff is one of these. Gorgeously succinct, entertaining and theoretically confident, her *Fag Hag* is a whistlestop autobiography of a Marseillaise's life lived on the '*outre-gauche*' or 'outer left' of France. This phrase, intended to bring to mind outer space, is Miesseroff's coinage for an archipelago of lesser-known anti-state communes and subversive experiments, from the naturist colonies of her childhood as the daughter of anarchist émigrés from Russia, to the Situationist-inspired insurrectionary gangs of her adult life in the environs of Aix-en-Provence and Paris. It's a world the author positions as 'beyond' the realms of all those more classic species of Marxist typically credited for the uprisings of the extended 1968 period. Anti-authoritarian, queer and transfeminist to the bone, Lola's people are 'vandals', rioters, orgiasts. Anecdotes abound of 'higgledy-piggledy' living arrangements and 'polysexual explosions' among motley crews squatting houses or 'sleeping under the stars'.

Notably, against prevailing assessments of historic solidarity between gay and women's liberation movements as an overwhelming failure, it is a central contention of the *fag/hag* dialogue that neither uprising could have happened without the other. Too rarely is it appreciated, for instance, that 'lesbians and prostitutes' make 'an historical sisterhood', in feminist sex-radical's Joan Nestle's terms. Likewise, 'Hocquenghem's theorization of male homosexual desire was facilitated by his embedding in the revolutionary strand of women's liberation' in the sixties and seventies. For its part, Miesseroff's anecdote-forward portrait of this period makes such interconnections and interdependencies seem like the most obvious and inevitable thing in the world. She nonetheless succeeds, on the whole, in steering clear of romanticisation. *Fag Hag* does not excise the bad moments from the 'enchanted parentheses' created by her fellow 'vandalist' communards, as for instance when 'one of our number drowned before our eyes in the Rhône'.

For all their intoxicated blunders and bravado, though, the outre-gauchistes appear in these pages as infinitely more honourable than those cliques of university-affiliated party radicals who responded to the neoliberal counterrevolution in the eighties by swiftly trading in (in Hocquenghem's memorable phrase) 'their Mao collars for the Rotary Club'. To be sure, membership in the propertarian regime of family values was granted to many formerly militant gays, even before the advent of 'equal marriage' legislation. But for the author of *Fag Hag*, relinquishing commitment to class war and care communisation in exchange for 'the posts, sinecures, and honours on offer' would be akin to clitoridectomy. In a 2023 interview with the writer and school teacher Gilles Dauvé, Miesseroff affirmed that 'The only deep structural contradiction is the one inherent to capitalism: the class antagonism that capitalism is based on' – yet her very next breath was this: 'Polysexuality is the ability to love whom we want and fuck freely with whomever we want without any gender distinction, but also, if we feel like it, to do it with several people at the same time.' From the Situationist International she learned, she said, to *oppose separation.*

Fag Hag is prole-, hag-, whore- and fag-identified, then, but this bone-deep insurgent identity is lived as much as possible as an anti-identity, oriented toward its own 'self-transcendence' in a future society wherein 'any need to claim a particular sexual orientation should disappear.' Pending the positive obsolescence of sex-radical politics, in other words, our heroine refuses all attempts to disembed those politics from anticapitalism. As a result, fag-hagdom becomes palpable, across dozens of anecdotes, as a refusal of identitarianism: a rejection of all attempts to separate lesbians' interests from faggots', feminism from gay liberation or even from men, men from childcare politics, and women from the struggle against the family-form. 'I shouted with all my might', Lola recounts of her first and last experience attending a Gouines Rouges (Red Dykes) feminist meeting in 1971, during which a FHAR queen in drag entered the room in search of a left-behind coat, only to be jeered at as a patriarchal intruder. Lola fetches the coat and bellows at the assembled sisterhood that 'the comrade was anything but an enemy', before storming out to buy 'him' a surely needed drink: 'end of conversation with these "red" lesbians".' On another occasion, a Women's Liberation Movement meeting 'led by bourgeois ideologues' fatally repels Miesseroff and her then-housemates Elsa and Annabelle, who try in vain to contest the 'single-sex nature of the assembly' by explaining that 'we lived in a group with men both straight and gay, that we could not imagine any struggle without them, and that for us the emancipation of women could not come about in isolation from the emancipation of everyone, all sexual tendencies included.'

The intuition that 'a transgressive sexuality [can] also be a political weapon' clearly came to Miesseroff extremely early in life via the example of the queer and trans leftists and antifascists in her parents' community of adults committed to the southern naturist lifestyle. From adolescence, her intimate comradely relationships are formed often with queer men, even as her deepest loves bind her to women. For example, in 1965, the eighteen-year-old Miesseroff forms a trio with Michel and Léo as a freshman at Aix university ('after the fashion of *Jules and Jim*, although I slept with neither of them'). It is Michel, as it happens, who dubs Lola a fag hag for the first time. Although reluctant to be 'pigeonholed' at this point, our heroine has to admit that she is a 'a magnet to men-loving men' – a 'fag catcher', in her mentor Alban's phrase. Everyone concurs with this, and even Lola's father boasts that their godless family contains, not Rita, Saint of Whores, but 'Lola, Saint of Fags'. The fact of the matter is, Lola simply experiences her position as a woman – a voraciously polyamorous non-trans working class bisexual, to be precise – as inseparable from the oppression of 'fags'.

The fag-hag relation is never overtly instrumental in her story. In terms of respectability, Miesseroff was far from a beard or cover for closeted individuals in her circles. Picture this: shortly after May 1968, Lola has joined an action committee in her parents' French Communist Party-controlled hometown of Aubagne: an unaligned revolutionary initiative begun by 'high schoolers, a few college students, and several workers.' There, she befriends Christian, a fifteen-year-old homosexual. Christian is a leading figure locally in the Trotsykist league JCR (Jeunesse Communiste Révolutionnaire), but Lola is giving him all kinds of unorthodox radical literature, such as Raoul Vaneigem's *The Revolution of Everyday Life* or the Situationist International pamphlet 'On the misery of student life' (*'De la misère en milieu étudiant'*). Soon enough, Christian is expelled from the JCR for associating with anarchistic elements – 'in other words, with me.' Clearly, Lola was a 'perverting' influence on her peers, if anything an anti-beard. Decades later, Lane-McKinley evokes a similar horizon when she reminisces about an arrangement she formed in middle school to be someone's beard: 'it was hetero drag for the both of us, not just for him.'

How should an anticapitalist person like Madeline, or Max, or me – raised in the nineties – relate to the memory of yesteryear's revolutionary potential today without falling into melancholy, or nostalgia, or the fantasy that one could somehow recreate irretrievable historic circumstances so as to repeat those bygone days' beautiful failures? Half a century on from the general strikes and mass street warfare of May '68, 'we have been taught to cope with the sense that revolution is unreachable', as M muses to M. (It is possible sometimes to infer who is Max and who is Madeline, but not always; the use of the initial is clearly a purposive transindividual blurring.) And yet, look, 2020 was a time of riotous uprising in the United States, starting at Minneapolis's 3rd police precinct, which fire then spread to hundreds of cities, at one point even forcing the president into a bunker. 'What's going on right now reminds me of previous moments of heightened possibility', writes the hag to the fag, or maybe vice versa, referencing the 2010 Oakland riots for Oscar Grant in which they both participated, while simultaneously gesturing at riots that took place before either of them was born. 'At the same time, there is a sense of unfamiliarity that I am more curious about.' Yes, responds the fag (or maybe the hag): 'The unfamiliarity of this moment is that now it's plain we'll need more than just a rupture to get us through.'

One consequence of this defamiliarising historic shift is an unmissable difference in tone between *fag/hag* and *Fag Hag*, for all the two texts' political affinities. For Miesseroff, the chronicling of the stormy career of a fag hag is a celebratory, proud, defiant matter, notwithstanding the memoirist's hopes that the world will one day transcend the need for those terms. In contrast, the whole fag/hag idea is characterised as limiting as much as promising by Fox and Lane-McKinley, for whom it is possibly frustrating more than anything else, a dialectic 'both parts utopian and anti-utopian', best understood as a symptom. 'This is not a fag/hagiography', the duo clarify in their preface. Rather, fag/hag is to be regarded as the 'archaic name' of a relationship still, alas, in play, which conceptually provides 'a foothold' on 'capitalism's continual reinvention in the name of "family".' Fags and hags, after all, are twinned outcasts from the political economy of heterosexuality. They have often and persistently nurtured embryonic anti-families together in the interstices of society, yet their self-definition *in relation* to that economy also means that their banding-together has privileged a coupling-up, one that reflects limits on the anti-familial imagination as much as a vision of another world.

Recall, for example, how the hags and fags of the long nineties – e.g., Julia Roberts or Madonna with Rupert Everett in *My Best Friend's Wedding* or *The Next Best Thing* – were always folding themselves into some kind of pseudo-nuptial or would-be-parental family narrative. Will and Grace became fixated on having a family, possibly with each other, and at the end of *Dawson's Creek*, the fag stepped in to father the dead hag's child. As Lane-McKinley and Fox put it: 'the threat of coupledom looms'. Only in 'moments of uprising' does this threat really recede, as far as M and M's 'actual experiences of political community' are concerned. Miesseroff's account of outer-left political community very much bears the latter insight out, insofar as the final sections of *Fag Hag* take an abrupt despondent turn because the author is addressing the relatively demobilised and anti-utopian left of 'that damnable decade', the eighties, and its long aftermath, a landscape she views as dominated by 'exclusionary' feminisms, 'fragmented identity politics', deeply unradical gay communitarianisms, and merely 'defensive' struggles.

In the 2020s, rearguard activism is sadly 'more necessary than ever' to defend minoritised populations' meagre freedoms, or so Miesseroff emphasises, 'but all the same, issue politics should in my opinion never be more than a stage – or rather an aspect – of the struggle against all forms of oppression.' For their part, Fox and Lane-McKinley may never have known an era anterior to the anti-utopian atmospheres of neoliberalism, but they still both know, from fragmentary firsthand knowledge of occupations and riots, that 'nothing compares to the miracle of social revolution.' An insurgency, writes Fox, is nothing less than a 'psychic transformation', a magic that supersedes so-called single issues, and 'nothing else will do' – even if, at least to date, there has always then followed 'the isolating work of keeping the memory of the miracle alive' in the depressing aftermath of defeat. On the other hand, in the other *Fag Hag*, we are offered an image of this labour as potentially non-isolating in an afterword by Hélène Hazéra, an erstwhile member of

'Les Gazolines', the trans break-off group from the FHAR. What if the onus to militate against forgetfulness, like the tending of a fire, could be collectively distributed? Lola's shared apartment was, Hazéra says, 'a place where the last live coals of the furnace of May 1968 still glowed.' The glow may nowadays be imperceptible to some, but there are still some who regard those live coals as an inheritance, a responsibility.

Pending the dissolution of these limiting categories, what could the hag aspire to be to the fag, the fag to the hag? In that *Salon* article, the category of friend was held up as the dignified option, a given. Are we sure, though, that we know what friendship is? For the late Chitty – about whom Lane-McKinley and Fox are lovingly talking in much of their correspondence – friendship was something that capitalism, homophobia, heterosexuality and the bourgeois family have killed. In a series of unpublished notes, tended to like embers by those he left behind, Christopher charged our society with the murder of 'the friend-as-lover', and linked the very possibility of doing politics, *revolutionary* politics, with the resurrection of this elusive promise he called the friend. Many readers will surely balk at the very construction 'friend-as-lover', let alone the premise of friendship as a utopian horizon not-even-yet-quite-graspable to us in the present. Our culture's tendency is to subordinate the terminology of friendship – as in the banal ubiquity of *friending* and the status demotion of *friendzoned* – to the more serious attachments of coupledom. That, surely, is why I feel it would be controversial to characterise the opposite-sex bond of the fag-hag duo in the aspirational terms of Chitty's mourned institution, 'the friend-as-lover'.

And yet! Lovers are not defined by their fucking. Lane-McKinley and Fox, throughout *fag/hag*, repeatedly unsettle their reader by asking us to countenance the liminal, antagonistic fag-hag relation as a kind of 'not-quite-heterosexuality' – a love that is 'not-quite-gay and not-quite-straight'. Furthermore, they insist that to strive toward loving friendship in this hell-world, whether on a fag-hag axis or otherwise, is no banal given, but a vertiginous task. It is vertiginous because the world we seek to bring into being because of our desire for one another's flourishing will necessarily make us into quite different people via a transformational leap; one devoutly to be wished, yet replete with loss. This is friendship, or, what Fox and Lane-McKinley call 'becoming other together'. What it paradoxically means is that true friends are those who muster willingness to one day leave each other (as well as their selves) behind.

As we enter the second Trump presidency in the West, we are witnessing a rash of separatist and micronationalist impulses among self-described gays and feminists. My intuition, in this moment, is to ask some of them what the horizon of superficially reasonable utterances like 'no to penises' or 'ladies, I'm not your gay boyfriend' is ultimately supposed to be. Like: sister, who made you the womanhood border-police vis-à-vis that queen looking for her coat? And, brother, how can you be so sure? Why not take a leaf out of Lola's book, loosen your grip on yourself, and try it? The reports of friendship's death are greatly exaggerated, one hopes. A horizon of friendlessness between feminized minorities and other sex/gender deviants remains as unimaginable to many of us 'feminists against cisness' (to borrow Emma Heaney's term) as it is, apparently, appealing to the various 'post-liberal' factions of contemporary gender politics, from queerphobic 'reactionary feminism' to the rise of (trans)misogynistic gay conservatism. If the fires of friendship have not quite been killed, however, Miesseroff, Lane-McKinley and Fox's animation of the fag-hag dialectic still point to the urgency of stoking them. Capitalism, I suspect, loves to see us unfriendly, on account of the friend's terrifying capacity to bring alive the substance of revolution in our hearts, compelling us to get together or, in other words, become other.

Sophie Lewis is the author of Enemy Feminisms: TERFs, Policewomen, and Girlbosses Against Liberation *(2025),* Abolish the Family: A Manifesto for Care and Liberation *(2022) and* Full Surrogacy Now: Feminism Against Family *(2019).*

Dossier: Marina Vishmidt, 1976-2024

Crystal drills
Marina Vishmidt, 1976-2024
Ray Brassier

To reduce Marina to her accomplishments as a thinker feels reductive, aping capitalism's reduction of human life to a single measurable activity, just as it feels presumptuous to 'assess' Marina's achievements, like an inspector brandishing a checklist. Yet it is primarily as a thinker and teacher that Marina was renowned so what I want to do here is not pretend to assess but simply to express my sense of her extraordinariness in both these domains. I witnessed Marina's unwavering dedication to her students last year when, already gravely ill, she devoted as much time to preparing her next class as to the conference paper she was about to deliver. In an academic climate where teaching is depreciated while 'indicators of esteem' like conference presentations are inflated, Marina's refusal to put her own prestige ahead of her students' needs speaks volumes about her personal and political integrity. Although I never saw her teach, I imagine her classes were like her thinking: boldly comprehensive without being domineering; sharply incisive but never dismissive, in accordance with her uncommonly generous and typically expansive ethos. Yet Marina's thinking was as exacting as it was magnanimous. Her writing is uncompromising in tracking dialectical complexity, which is another way of describing the pursuit of truth. *Speculation as a Mode of Production* is an exceptional work whose full import, both political and philosophical, will be reckoned for years to come.[1] It twins art and value, aesthetic uselessness and socioeconomic utility under the rubric of speculation, which governs the logic of aesthetic subtraction from economic value as well as the valorisation of this subtraction. Speculation in this sense names the stage of capitalist production which commensurates useful exchange and useless inexchangeability. 'What happens', asks Marina, 'when both use and uselessness are sublated into the form of the speculative? Such an indistinction, as it obtains for labour and for art, can be held to be symptomatic of barriers to accumulation reached by the speculative mode of production, as well as the forms of antagonism that can arise from this impasse.'[2] Marina's determination to draw out the new modes of political antagonism arising from the metamorphoses of social contradiction is as typical of her as it should be exemplary for others. It made her matchless as a theorist but also somewhat exceptional among connoisseurs of *Wertkritik* too often content to chide activist 'naivety'. Yet there was nothing remotely naive about Marina's unwavering commitment to what she called 'antisystemic activism', in which antagonisms of race, class and gender are necessarily intertwined through the metamorphoses of value. Marina's political militancy was at one with her theoretical stringency. Complexity was not a license for equivocation, just as the inextricability of conceptual and political contradiction was no excuse for evading commitment. If she was dogged in pursuing dialectical truth, it is because she could detect the muffled pulse of liberation in even the most rebarbative theoretical or aesthetic works. At a moment when Israel's genocide of Palestinians has exposed the ignominious sophistry of certain proponents of *Wertkritik*, Marina's emphatic public solidarity with

Palestinian liberation was both inspiring and courageous, especially since she was teaching in Austria, a country where anti-Palestinian sentiment is perhaps even more virulent than Germany. It was Marina's fidelity to what is sometimes disparaged as 'historical materialism', the insistence that new forms of domination engender new possibilities of resistance, that let her see how changes in art's relation to capital are indissociable from mutations in capital's relation to labor. Once negativities like uselessness and inexchangeability become provinces of value accumulation, art can no longer be juxtaposed to capital as harbinger of non-identity. This makes it necessary to revise a longstanding Adornian consensus about art's negative relation to value:

> If Adorno's negative dialectics of the social ontology of art presupposes instrumental reason and the monopoly of ratio (as exchange-value) as the regime of heteronomy that art, with its open-ended, future-figuring and material speculation was in principle opposed to, we now have to assess a situation in which the development of capital's value forms and value relations have captured much of this speculative energy, affirming processes which Adorno saw as antithetical to capital altogether.[3]

For Marina, this capture of art's speculative energy is misdiagnosed by institutional critique, which attributes it to private capital's grip on galleries and museums. But art's capture is not merely institutional, it occurs in the very production of subjectivity from whence social roles like that of artist, curator, or critic originate. Marina proposed 'infrastructural critique' as a corrective to critique which flatter art's fantasy of autonomy by ascribing its heteronomy to institutionalisation. She defines infrastructure as 'the spatial articulation of historically specific social relations which persists over time.'[4] It is not just a set of objects – buildings, spaces, equipment, amenities, and the labour required to maintain them – but a system of social relations, distributed across space and stretching over time, embodied in the relations among these objects. The point of infrastructural critique is not simply to expose the nexus of relations involving exploitation and domination occluded by art as institution but to reveal the facticity of these social relations as that which enables the disruption as well as the maintenance of art's participation in capitalist production. This tension is the index of critical negativity proper to infrastructural critique, whose political import for Marina does not reside in endless debates about protocols of representation but in antagonism waged from the standpoint of social transformation. As she puts it: 'infrastructure is both the basis for miserable and distorted life and the resource for very different types of co-ordination, along with the subjectivities that would struggle to realise them.'[5]

Beyond its import for aesthetic theory, *Speculation as a Mode of Production* also contains piercing insights into value theory. The commodification of abstract 'employability', beyond any specific modality of employment, turns the latency of unemployed but potentially employable labour-power into a new source of surplus-value. The potency of *Arbeitsvermögen*, labour-capacity, which for some Autonomist Marxists figures a creative capacity that transcends labour-power's use-value for commodity production, becomes just another commodified resource. With this shift, it is not just the actuality of labour that is exploited but its possibility:

> We ... witness a change in the relationship between potentiality as the content of labour-power and labour as the substance of value. Potentiality takes on a different socio-economic standing altogether when 'employability' becomes a commodity with its own lucrative industry of government contracts, in a context where it is unclear whether it is the labour market or the welfare budget that is shrinking more rapidly. When work-readiness rather than work becomes both the carrot and the stick in the state management of expanding pools of the structurally unemployed, it is clear that speculative labour is not simply a way of emphasising the potentiality of non-realisation in all cases of labour-power sold for a wage, but the means for harvesting value from labour power which cannot find a buyer.[6]

Unemployment becomes a commodifiable resource at the point where the actuality of labour's unemployed potency falls under the aegis of value. The full ramifications of this remarkable insight have yet to be taken up and in this regard Marina's work has decisively influenced my own. Still more remarkable is the fact that a thinker so profound could also be so prolific: besides *Speculation as a Mode of Production*, Marina's collected works comprise several co-edited books, dozens of articles, chapters, and numerous miscellaneous interventions ranging over twenty-five years.[7] Collaboration was a persistent feature of her work, showing how she was willing to contribute her exceptional power as a thinker to collective endeavours whose worth cannot be calculated by institutional metrics.

I began by saying I would not try to assess Marina's achievements yet all I've spoken about is her work. But I also knew Marina, first when she was a graduate student and subsequently as an increasingly formidable theorist. I mention this because what is extraordinary in Marina's work derives from what was extraordinary about her person. She was luminously intelligent, deeply principled, and profoundly kind, by which I do not mean 'agreeable' but full of care for thinking and acting rightly. Of course, to highlight her virtues in this way is to abstract from her humour, her playfulness, her love of mischief and irony; everything which made her lovable rather than some stern incarnation of virtue (a suggestion which would surely make her laugh). To say that her loss is incalculable for those who knew and loved her is to resort to a necessary cliché. We are all diminished by her premature death. If she honoured friends with kindness, she honoured readers with difficulty. She was too principled to court academic celebrity, yet her achievements – prematurely cut short – will outlast that of more feted contemporaries because they will stand as a common resource of intellectual wealth for years to come.

Notes

1. Marina Vishmidt, *Speculation as a Mode of Production: Forms of Value Subjectivity in Art and Capital* (Brill: Leiden and Boston, 2018).
2. Vishmidt, *Speculation*, 25.
3. Vishmidt, *Speculation*, 24.
4. Marina Vishmidt, 'Only as Self-Relating Negativity: Infrastructure and Critique', *Journal of Science and Technology of the Arts* 13:3 (2021), 15.
5. Vishmidt, 'Self-Relating', 20.
6. Vishmidt, *Speculation*, 20.
7. They have been made available online here: https://onvishmidt.memoryoftheworld.org/.

Against running in place
The speculative thought of Marina Vishmidt
Zoe Sutherland

... an angry, loving detachment from what keeps us running in place.[1]

Up until the end, Marina brought things to life. She was an animist, of sorts. She treated objects with the serious playfulness of a small child, our Zoom chats and collaborative work sessions punctuated with the animation of ornaments and stuffed toys. Nothing was allowed to stay inert; nothing was sealed off. Her desire for more collective ways of being – evidenced by her countless friendships, camaraderies and collaborations – was unwavering. She was social glue and social animator, mobilising the ever-expanding web of people who gravitated towards her into creative and intellectual projects. To be in dialogue with Marina felt like conversing with, or participating in the assemblage of, a world. An academic by pay cheque – and by all accounts, an inspiring and challenging teacher – she reviled the individualism and competitiveness rewarded by the field, refusing to overidentify with, or claim ownership over, ideas, creative projects or texts. For Marina, process was everything and collaboration was key, so long as they were adequately antagonistic in just the right ways.

Most evidently, Marina animated concepts and methodological frameworks. Highly suspicious of 'theoretical closures and inflations of all kinds',[2] she had a commitment to negative dialectical thinking and a sensitivity to the resonances between disciplinary approaches, always striving to substantiate these at the systematic level. Secure in her intellectual and political sensibilities, she was open to pursuing diverse lines of thought. As Kerstin Stakemeier so beautifully captured, Marina had 'an acute and unrelenting dedication to dropping nothing that had ever emerged as a product of revolutionary sense(s)',[3] and through this, things took shape. A difficult thinker to keep up with, Marina's commitment to staying with dialectical complexity was not a stylistic matter, but a means of resisting the reification of political horizons through easy affirmations or abstract negations. For Marina, reading, writing – and political organising – should 'shatter and reconstitute' us.[4] Influenced greatly by Adorno, but always seeking to move beyond the self-imposed limitations of his critique, Marina's more promiscuous method brought together a diverse constellation of discourses – philosophy, materialist feminism, political economy, radical ecology, contemporary art and poetry, critical black studies and finance, to name a few – to produce an ever-moving object of analysis. Negative dialectical thinking, immanent as it is to its object, was, for Marina, a form of play at its most political. It was a way of preventing a 'running in place', and a means of remaking the subject, but also the world, through the 'exhilaration of negation of a violent and necrotic social stasis.'[5]

Marina's theoretical project is not easily summarised, not least because it is unfinished. She was an immensely prolific writer, whose work exists largely as an abundance of – mostly commissioned – essays, articles or talks, with only two monographs.[6] Generally opposed to fixed definitions, her arguments resist encapsulation into an overly neat or abstract formula. But if Marina's writings provide a set of prompts and provocations for others to take forwards, it is as much in her approach to critique, as in the specific details of her analysis.

Marina had been exploring the relation between art, labour, capital, and reproduction, from at least the early 2000s, most notably in *Mute*. But the 2008 global financial crisis and its resulting anti-austerity struggles, alongside related theoretical developments of the time, impacted her thinking in several ways. I first met Marina at a series of weekly meetings in London – the 'Social Crisis Social' – in which an ever-increasing group of us tried to grapple with the implications of the crisis and its fallout. We became friends, soon to live around the corner from each other in Hackney. The resurgence of interest in materialist feminism after 2008 inspired the formation of the London-based Feminist Reading Group in 2012, of which we were both participants. Marina was enticed by the debates within communisation theory in the early 2010's – most notably those between *Theorie Communiste,* Maya Andrea Gonzalez and *Endnotes* – which strengthened a 'negative' turn in left feminist discourse by conceptualising gender as a 'social form' to be abolished.[7] As Danny Hayward explains, the proliferation of riots, general strikes, port blockades and occupations of public squares in the post-crisis years led Marina to come up against the limits of her post-autonomist orientation towards the 'generalisation' of reproductive struggles into state institutions, an echo of the 'social factory'.[8] It also revitalised debates around logistics, capitalist infrastructure and technology, all of which shaped her thinking. Drawn to the 'negativity' of these theories, Marina became sceptical of what she saw as a latent automaticity at work within their thinking, a faith that revolution would result from some grand rupture. Debates around the validity of theories of 'subsumption', culminating in a 2014 workshop in Bilbao, 'What is to Be Done Under Real Subsumption', provided a framework through which Marina began engaging critically with the abstract conclusions of much theory of the time. It is possible to detect a more politically situated, strategic turn in Marina's thinking, following this workshop, fuelled by a desire to push past the seemingly inherent aporias in much revolutionary thought, and to avoid a form of thinking that 'weaves ontological spells against the urgency of specific tasks of transformation.'[9] The subsequent conceptual and theoretical approaches Marina developed aimed to establish a materialist praxis of determinate negation.

Speculation

As Hayward notes, Marina's attraction to counter-intuitive and negatively recursive thinking would lead her towards a theory of capital as a system that defines itself through exceptions; a Marxism thought from the perspective of its limits or outsides.[10] In 2022, Marina claimed that if there was anything systematic about her work, it was the pursuit of 'a non-functionalist and non-ontological' – rather a dialectical – understanding of the 'constitutive exception' to the operation of the rule under capital.[11] The categories of 'art' and 'unwaged reproductive labour' recur and rebound throughout her work as key exceptions. In her 2018 monograph *Speculation as a Mode of Production: Forms of Value Subjectivity in Art and Capital*, Marina developed the concept of 'speculation' as a revision of Adorno's claims about the autonomy of art. Under conditions of contemporary capital – with its financialised logics, and precarious forms of labour – art can no longer be considered absolutely other to labour, with a 'capitalist modernity-directed divine impotence (autonomy) as the source of its critical force.'[12] Instead, a parallel can be discerned between contemporary capital and contemporary art, as they constitute 'the poles of a society structured around speculation, reflected in social practices ranging from systems of welfare provision to the constitution of the self and the image of work.'[13] In an inversion of Adorno's problematic, Marina traced the 'speculative form of labour' within both art and finance. Drawing upon Steven Shaviro's work on 'open' and 'closed' speculation, she argues that financial speculation, typically considered 'open' in the sense that it creates wealth and markets, can also be seen as 'closed'. As self-valorising, it produces nothing but more of itself, positing 'no horizon besides an indefinite replication of the future as present, thus predicated on enclosing the future as temporality and resource.'[14] The open-endedness of financial speculation ultimately 'stabilises' itself on other levels of the system geared to generate profit. At the same time, the 'open' speculative potential of art – 'proposing new worlds' and 'renewing perception' – is imbricated in the 'closed' speculation of the financial market, and the 'disciplinary autonomy' that defines them as 'constitutively 'free' of real-world consequences.'[15]

Art both mediates and is mediated by speculative capital and its ability to be 'socially speculative' emerges in processes of 'dis-identification, exacerbation and singularization'.[16] Speculation is thus not a concept denoting pure open-endedness in its orientation to the future, but contains a 'negativity' in that it is constituted by antagonism and contestation. Critical art practice must grapple with this entanglement if it is to avoid the reification resulting from the work's confinement within an aesthetic form, and must enable an 'immanent connection to unpredictable processes of 'determinate social transformation'.[17] Art cannot deepen its political commitment by trying to deny or escape its autonomous character, dissolving art into life or social practice, but only by reducing its claims to autonomy through the 'deconstruction of those mechanisms that establish and maintain "the artistic" as different from other social practices.'[18] As Anthony Iles puts it, to deepen its immanent critique, art must work through 'negating by making unbearably present the contradictory ground of its apparent autonomy.'[19] It is in this sense that speculation is, for Marina, the 'negative dialectics of artistic autonomy.'[20]

Photo by Michael Runyan

Social reproduction and gender

Marina mobilised this dialectically negative approach within her feminist thinking, as a means of avoiding political horizons that become reified into positions of simple affirmations or abstract negations. These affirmative and negative tendencies often figure in her work as the 'politics of reproduction' on the one hand, and 'gender abolition' on the other. The politics of reproduction – of which Silvia Federici is often the model – is driven by a latent workerist impulse to extend the 'myth of the revolutionary subject' in a feminist direction. It demands visibility and recognition for reproductive labour, defending it from its capitalist devaluation by claiming that it is necessary to value production after all. Its valorisation of the reproductive – sometimes invoking romanticised images of subsistence economies – implies and perpetuates the separability of reproduction from production, and gendered labour from its overall position in the reproduction of capital. Taking the concept of reproduction, which Marx was using at a high level of abstraction and generality, and mapping it onto a designated set of concrete tasks characterised by replacement and maintenance, Marina saw some strands of Marxist feminism as having lost sight of an analysis of the position of gendered labour from the standpoint of the social totality. Once dislocated, reproduction can be held up as the positive, salvageable half of the capitalist whole, rather than an aspect of the mode of production to be analysed from the standpoint of its elimination. But Marina's concern was as much practical as conceptual: grounding a politics in reproduction *per se*, in abstraction from any socially transformative process, can end up suppressing the need and desire for more radical change, privileging maintenance, continuity and survival: in current conditions, a form of crisis management. The politics of reproduction can end up with a position that moralises gendered labour, along with gender itself. In a similar way to some manifestations of the 'politics of care', this approach constructs reproductive labour, and gender, not as a 'concrete historical experience to be negated', but as a 'metaphysical principle to be affirmed'.[21] Lacking attention to 'non-identity thinking', certain forms of feminist thought and politics unwittingly seal up any potential 'space of negation'.[22]

In contrast to the affirmative impulse of the politics of reproduction, arguments for gender abolition – associated for Marina with communisation theory – understands gender to be a social form. As such, the political horizons that emerge out of organising around it are themselves 'form-determined by the real abstractions to be done away with'.[23] Due to the logical connection between gender and the capitalist form of value, a feminism based upon the affirmation of gender and gendered roles cannot be transformative. Instead, women must eradicate the very ground upon which they stand and abolish themselves *as women*. Inspired by the *Endnotes* text 'The Logic of Gender', Marina was initially enticed by the theory of gender abolition, but came to think that *taken on its own* it was inadequately materialist. Following an exchange with Ray Brassier in the subsumption workshop, she named an inherent 'paradox of subjectivity' within the theory of self-abolition: the collective subject of abolition comes into being through the struggle that abolition entails, but has to eliminate its ground in the society the movement wants to change or overcome'.[24] This poses a logical problem: who is the subject that initiates and who comes out of the other side? But importantly, it also poses a practical one: how can a self that is defined negatively – constituted by the capital relation – find resources to negate that relation or struggle for something else? Avoiding the affirmative impulse of the politics of reproduction, the virtue of the theory of gender abolition for Marina is that it 'operates by way of determinate negation, setting its horizon within the immanence of struggle'. Instead of an abstract dismissal of certain elements of the present, its negative critique proceeds determinately from 'the structural role of gender within the reproduction of the system', paying attention to the shape that takes historically.[25] But while the analysis is a determinate one, without an adequate account of subjectivity and subjectivation, the imperative to 'abolish' remains abstract.[26]

Marina identified a feedback loop between affirmation and negation in radical thought; the desire to affirm produces its opposite: the temptation to abolish. But 'neither can be materialist as long as what they really want to do is escape.'[27] The subject cannot be found through 'identity thinking' nor 'wished away' through theoretical ruptures; only overcome through a living, social praxis, which necessarily unfolds as 'painful contradiction'.[28] The capital relation might be the social horizon of the reproduction of identities, but this horizon is not totalising; it is contradictory and constitutively incomplete.[29] Thought may need to identify, as Adorno tells us, but identity thinking must turn against itself: it must dis-identify. Marina's dialectically negative praxis allows social locations to be 'politically and theoretically read as structural without thereby being read as functional or integral', and for difference to be construed as 'a nonreified social experience that has political significance open to determination and inflection in situated emancipatory struggles.'[30] They appear as the products of relations of subjects and objects in transformative processes. In a 2018 dialogue with Hayward, Marina describes negativity as both 'vehicular' – a way of getting somewhere – and an 'impossible horizon'. If we cannot simply escape – if the only way out is through – then what is required is the 'interminable movement' of a rigorously materialist form of negative dialectical practice, one which doesn't 'polarise radical imagination from radical action.' Negativity must strive to link radical thought to its material conditions, 'keeping that horizon fractured and also introverted in such a way that there is never a guarantee of legitimacy.'[31] This lay at the heart of Marina's formulation of 'infrastructural critique'.

Infrastructural critique

From the mid-2010s, inspired by multiple sources – 'transversally-minded art-activist practices' of the 1990s, theories of race and colonialism, and debates around logistics, technology and capitalist infrastructure – Marina developed an 'infrastructural critique' which will continue to influence art theory and practice, as well as debates around organisational strategy, for years to come. The 'infrastructural' is a multi-layered concept, which gathers complexity as it develops through her work and, like 'speculation', describes both a field of study and method of critique. As a field of study, 'infrastructure' is another way of conceptualising the material conditions required for an institution to exist and be reproduced; that which persists and makes possible, but also makes *impossible* certain forms of social life and subjectivity. Marina would increasingly come to draw upon work from the black radical tradition to theorise infrastructure as the material basis for violent processes of racialisation and extraction and to think through the necropolitical role of infrastructural coercion and neglect.[32] As a committed anti-Zionist, the catastrophic destruction of infrastructure in Gaza, in addition to the direct slaughtering of Palestinians, would have stood out in her final years as a horrifying example of this. But for Marina, the concept of infrastructure is polyvalent. It refers to the objects, tools and equipment that are key to reproducing the capitalist social world and its institutions – bridges, tunnels, sewers, pipelines, telecommunication wires –

and to the labour and expertise they embody. While these material determinations set parameters for action, they are at the same time 'crystallisations' and 'negative imprints' of social forms, in the words of an *Endnotes* text she admired.[33] Marina also saw infrastructure as 'the articulation of the historically specific social relations which persists over time',[34] exploring how the speculative force of art – and political struggle – can clarify, open up and repurpose those infrastructures for other ends.

While Marina's orientation to the 'infrastructural' developed over time, her starting point was a critical engagement with the 'institutional critique' of art, and it is from here that we can begin to unpick the political stakes of this concept. The shift from institutional to infrastructural critique, Marina tells us, is a shift from a standpoint that accepts the institution as a horizon, to one which understands it as 'a historical and contingent nexus of material conditions amenable to rearrangement through struggle and different forms of inhabitation and dispersal.'[35] An example of institutional critique she uses is the now canonical site-specific work of Michael Asher. In an untitled work of 1973 at the Galleria Franco Toselli, Asher sandblasted the walls of an empty gallery space to reveal layers of rough material texture, peeling off the 'white cube' surface of the representational space and producing the effect of a derelict warehouse. In another untitled work at the Claire Copley Gallery (1974), he removed the partition in an otherwise empty gallery to reveal the small administrative office in the corner, in which an administrator was working. Asher sought to de-mystify art, Marina tells us, by disclosing its commodity character or intimacy with private or speculative capital, by way of foregrounding the enabling container of representation; the gallery or museum. While Marina remained compelled by the inherent reflexivity of institutional critique, she saw it as

Photo by Michael Runyan

a recuperation of social struggles of the 1970s back into the art institution, producing a form of reflexivity that is ultimately too comfortable and contemplative. Limited to acts of self-exposure, its immanent critique of the spaces of artistic exhibition and discourse rests at highlighting the 'social and symbolic parameters' of the institution via the physical fabric and material space. By confining itself to the representational space, it accepts and reproduces the 'moralising premises' that perpetuate it, preserving its frame as a condition of legitimacy. Without moving beyond this gesture of making visible – in this case, what is already known – the 'horizon of disclosure' *per se* is valorised and held up as normative for art: we are left with an art, and a form of critique, that can 'point' but not 'grab'. When the 'legitimate' bounds of art's critical potential become circumscribed in this way, artists are essentially left identifying with their target of critique, as well as their position within relations of production. Artists are brought together with the institution in a 'half-hearted *tableau vivant* of autonomy', inflating the 'phantom power' of autonomous art and allowing a flow of critical 'capital' back into the institution.[36] When art is reified as an exceptional space of freedom, its dependence upon massive and wide-ranging practices of extraction and social injustice is obfuscated and the 'desire for the political in the field of art' is captured and bent towards affirmation and repetition of these violent practices.[37] How might art move beyond this paradox in which, as Andrea Fraser puts it, the 'institution of critique' becomes co-extensive with the 'institution of art'?[38] What are the conditions of possibility under which art and critique might actualise their grabbing potential? How to keep that horizon fractured and introverted?

Infrastructural critique, Marina tells us, would take an immanent view on the means of production or conditions of possibility of both the institution and its critique.[39] In an unusually biographical register during her 2022 Arnheim lecture at the Humboldt, Marina described how her work had always been in some way or another about 'conditions of possibility', detailing how participating in Riot Grrrl and DIY zine culture in the 1990s laid the ground for her thinking about art and politics by demonstrating how forms of organising were as important as any artistic product – the distinction being a 'relatively contingent matter of practice'.[40] While Kant established transcendental conditions for knowledge, tracing the 'legitimate' limits of reason – defining the possible, by demarcating the impossible – the idea accrues a more 'concrete' register in Marina's work. *Material* 'conditions of possibility' include the 'existence of a demarcated field of practice' *and* practices that transpire within – and traverse in and out of – that field. They thus imply 'conditions of legibility' for practices, and a field's composition 'along the vectors of objective and subjective determination by race, class, gender and relation to the law.'[41] Given Marina's interest in Deleuze and Guattari whose ideas run through her texts, often implicitly, it also includes the formation of subjectivity through the social organisation and orientation of desire under capitalist value relations. To understand conditions of possibility as concrete, is to avoid pre-given abstractions – e.g. the 'institutional' – and reconstruct the object in all its complexity and contingency. Conditions of possibility are both prerequisites for knowledge, desire, hope or action, and the materially determinate products of it, meaning they are plastic and malleable.

Given the deep and multi-layered nature of these conditions, how can we conceptualise this malleability? Foucault's inversion of the Kantian problematic asks: 'in what is given to us as universal, necessary, obligatory, what place is occupied by whatever is singular, contingent, and the product of arbitrary constraints?'[42] What appear as transcendental conditions can be revealed as historical and contingent – made possible by their own set of conditions – and, in doing so, the contingencies, exceptions or breakage points can be gleaned. Marina would appreciate this recursive softening of the boundary between 'conditions' and 'production', but wouldn't stop at puncturing the illusion of the necessity of these limits. Instead, she wants to

> forget about insides and outsides as Kantian 'what it is possible for us to know, what is it possible for us to hope' ... as limits or borders for us, and take them up as productive equipment afforded by the field of art both economically and ideologically.[43]

Material conditions can be mobilised and weaponised against the 'field', 'turning that border into a chalk drawing on the pavement around a defunct institution' and, drawing on Fred Moten, 'taking it as a space for our "plans"'.[44] Reflexivity thus gains a materialist register; from the reflexivity of the contemplative subject, to one

of the conditions being mobilised as the tools and objects of action.

To avoid the 'comfort zone of reflexivity' art must do more than point out further infrastructural layers of the institution. It must operate 'transversally' to its institutional grammar, across representational and material realms and registers with the aim of mobilising and repurposing them. Marina saw the work of Cameron Rowland, which explores how juridical, cultural and financial artefacts and infrastructures reveal continuing profiting from colonialism and slavery, as one example. In *Encumbrance* (2020) at the ICA, Rowland carried out a re-mortgaging of the mahogany fittings obtained by the royal building as part of colonial trade. In *Disgorgement* (2016) they established an insurance trust – The Reparations Purpose Trust – held in the name of Artist's Space that bought shares in the Aetna insurance company. This company, that sold insurance to slaveowners, would pay out in the event of federal financial repayments for chattel slavery in the US. For Marina, Rowland's art practices move beyond a simple critique of the institution as property to identify the wider apparatus of racialised capitalism as a 'spectrum of real abstractions' – value, property, race. At the same time, by mobilising them at the level of function, the work enacts a desire for reparation by introducing 'friction' into the 'valorisation pathways of contemporary art'.[45] Rowland's practices don't just point to the art institution's role in the continued reproduction of the colonial and capital relation. Rather, they deconstruct the material or infrastructural conditions of autonomous art by materialising its contradictory ground, inserting itself within 'the gap between the institution's gestural benevolence and material violence.'[46] Rowland's works enact what Marina – in reference to Saidiya Hartmann – calls a 'burdened materialism'.[47] They move between the speculative form and empirical realism by working on real-life infrastructure as 'enabling constraints' for inequality, profit and death.

While art cannot escape its autonomous character through dissolving itself into social or political practice, infrastructural critique can occur through labour struggles and social antagonisms that keep a 'double focus' within and beyond the institution. Marina was connected to the 2018 protests and picket against the new campus art centre, the Goldsmith's Centre of Contemporary Art (GCCA), focusing on the labour conditions of the racialised migrant cleaners, who were outsourced to a private firm. She was also interested in the articulation of BDS, Fuck the Police, anti-displacement and Decolonize This Place militants at the Whitney, and their conjunction with the social antagonisms of museum and biennial staff. 'Transversal' art practices can give rise to 'speculative alliances' between diverse actors who are brought together not through some form of positive identification, but negatively – through recognition that the same forces are destroying their lives. Such art practices, Marina argues, tend to relate to the art institution as an exemplary but ultimately contingent space of capitalist reproduction, which protects against an overidentification with that institution's recuperative logics. Social and political movements that mobilise identity categories in order to stake out antagonism rather than to claim sameness – movements of non-identity – can thus 'deflect the reification of boundaries in practice' without completely dissolving the delimitation necessary for the identification of resources that might enable strategic thinking. By politicising rather than denying 'socially effective differences' and inscribing these through and within determinate social spaces, 'cuts' and 'breathing holes' can be made that reveal something about the material conditions for transformation. A shift to infrastructural critique represents a desire to mediate the closures and inflations, both theoretically and practically, 'focusing the link between the material and ideological conditions of the institution of art in a way that de-centres rather than affirms it.'[48]

Marina was part of a growing group of global thinkers trying to rearticulate the continuing relevance of critical theory and critique. Whatever she was writing about, it was always, at the same time, an investigation into the material possibilities of critique, and a reflection upon the form that critique should take today. If, in its philosophical origins, critique is an analysis of 'conditions of possibility', then critique itself must have conditions of possibility – 'materially infrastructural', rather than epistemological – which can be examined through the same process.[49] Critical theory must always be prepared to turn its thinking upon itself, as Marina often did. Most notably, she acknowledged how her developing interest in critical Black studies had forced her to rethink her earlier genealogy of capitalist and aesthetic forms, demonstrating that modernity and modern art couldn't be grasped adequately without foregrounding processes of dispossession and dehumanisation.[50] Her interest in critique was also an interest in the formation of subjectivities for emancipatory ends. She believed that an infrastructural mode of critique could work against the 'unconditional autonomy of the isolated European-identified Enlightenment subject', which has informed most debates in radical theory, and could instead help to reanimate a side-lined history of critique as 'a material practice of antagonism whose subject, if it has one, is dispersive, uncategorisable and collective.'[51]

In her final years, Marina refused to dwell upon her illness. She had no interest in reifying what she saw as the 'contingency of cells' into an identity, and rejected the claim that some deeper meaning for her life could be unearthed through grappling with her own mortality. There would be no overly simple reconciliation. Instead, she continued reading, writing and giving talks, animating bats, and clams, and hedgehogs.

Notes

1. This is taken from a quote in a text written for a 2017 film produced by Channels, a feminist artmaking collective in which Marina participated.
2. From Marina Vishmidt, 'Speculation to Infrastructure: Material and Method in the Politics of Contemporary Art', Arnheim Lecture at Humboldt, 2022.
3. Kerstin Stakemeier, 'Marina's Cue's', in *e-flux Notes* (May 2024).
4. Marina Vishmidt, 'Art, Value, Subjects, Reasons. Some Aspects of Speculation as Production' in Simon Baier and Markus Klammer, eds., *Aesthetics of Equivalence* (Berlin: August Verlag, 2023), 112.
5. Marina Vishmidt and Andreas Petrossiants, 'Spaces of Speculation: Movement Politics in the Infrastructure', and interview for *Historical Materialism* (2020), available at: https://www.historicalmaterialism.org/spaces-of-speculation-movement-politics-in-the-infrastructure/.
6. Marina Vishmidt, *Speculation as a Mode of Production: Forms of Value Subjectivity in Art and Capital* (Leiden: Brill, 2018); Kerstin Stakemeier and Marina Vishmidt, *Reproducing Autonomy: Work, Money, Crisis and Contemporary Art* (London: Mute Publishing, 2016). An anthology of Marina's writings on infrastructural critique is forthcoming as Marina Vishmidt, *Infrastructural Critique: between Reproduction and Abolition* (London: Verso, 2026).

7. See Roland Simon, 'Distinction de Genres, Programmitisme et Communisation' in *Théorie Communiste* (2010); Maya Andrea Gonzalez, 'Communization and the Abolition of Gender' in Benjamin Noys, ed., *Communization and its Discontents: Contestation, Critique and Contemporary Struggles* (Brooklyn: Autonomedia, 2011); P. Valentine, 'The Gender Distinction in Communization Theory, *LIES* 1 (2012); Endnotes, 'The Logic of Gender', in *Endnotes 3: Gender, Race, Class and Other Misfortunes* (2013).
8. Danny Hayward, 'A Life Lived in Different Circumstances', forthcoming in *Variant* (2025).
9. Marina Vishmidt, from an unpublished interview with Thomas Watson conducted in 2023.
10. Hayward, 'A Life Lived'.
11. Marina Vishmidt, 'Externality and Necessity in Marxist and Ecological Concepts in Political Theory', delivered as an introduction at a workshop of the same name at York Political Theory Workshop, University of York, 2022.
12. Vishmidt, 'Spaces of Speculation'.
13. Vishmidt, 'Art, Value, Subjects, Reasons', 120.
14. Vishmidt, 'Spaces of Speculation'.
15. Ibid.
16. Vishmidt, 'Art, Value, Subjects, Reasons', 123.
17. Vishmidt, 'Spaces of Speculation'.
18. Stefan Germer, 'Haacke, Broodthaers, Beuys', *October* 45 (1989), 5. Thanks to Anthony Iles for pointing out Marina's enduring affection for this quote.
19. Anthony Iles, 'Plastic Givens: Speculation, Antagonism and Recursion in Unfinished Work with Marina Vishmidt, a talk given at Historical Materialism Conference, London, 2024.
20. Vishmidt, 'Spaces of Speculation'.
21. Marina Vishmidt, 'The Paradox of Self-Abolition: A Mapping Exercise', in *May* 16 (2016), 32.
22. This form of critique appears in many of Marina's texts. See for example 'Known Nowheres', in Ines Doujak & Oliver Ressler, eds, *Utopian Impulse: Flares in the Darkroom* (London: Pluto Press, 2015); 'Two Reproductions in (Feminist) Art and Theory since the 1970s', in *Third Text* 31: 1 (2017).
23. Vishmidt, 'The Paradox of Self-Abolition', 27.
24. Ray Brassier, 'Wandering Abstraction', *Mute Magazine* (2014). While Marina agreed with Brassier's critique of the logical paradox of self-abolition, she rejected his emphasis upon cognition and reason as the ultimate driver of revolutionary overcoming.
25. Vishmidt and Hayward, 'Self-Dissolution', 8.
26. Vishmidt, 'The Paradox of Self-Abolition', 32.
27. Vishmidt, 'Known Nowheres' 125.
28. Vishmidt and Hayward, 'Self-Dissolution', 9.
29. Marina Vishmidt and Zoe Sutherland, '(Un)making Value: Reading Social Reproduction Through the Question of Totality', in Kevin Floyd, Jen Hedler Phillis and Sarika Chandra, eds, *Totality Inside Out: Rethinking Crisis and Conflict under Capital* (New York: Fordham University Press, 2022), 85.
30. Ibid.
31. Vishmidt and Hayward, 'Self-Dissolution', 35-36.
32. Marina draws upon the work of Ruth Wilson Gilmore and Zandi Sherman.
33. Endnotes, 'Error', in *Endnotes 5: The Passions and the Interests* (Glasgow: Bell & Bain, 2019).
34. Marina Vishmidt, 'Only as Self-Relating Negativity: Infrastructure and Critique', *Journal of Science and Technology of the Arts* 13:3 (2021), 15.
35. Vishmidt, 'Only as Self-Relating Negativity', 14.
36. Marina Vishmidt, 'Beneath the Atelier, the Desert: Critique, Institutional and Infrastructural', in Tom Holert and Maria Hlavajova, eds, *Marion von Osten: Once We Were Artists* (A BAK Critical Reader in Artists' Practice) (Amsterdam: Valiz, 2017), 219.
37. Vishmidt, 'Spaces of Speculation'.
38. Andrea Fraser, 'From the Critical Institutions to the Institution of Critique', *Artforum* 44:1 (September 2005).
39. Vishmidt, 'Only as Self-Relating Negativity', 14.
40. Vishmidt, 'From Speculation to Infrastructure'.
41. Ibid.
42. Michel Foucault, 'What is Enlightenment, *The Foucault Reader* (New York: Pantheon Books, 1984), 45.
43. Vishmidt, 'Spaces of Speculation'.
44. Stefano Harney and Fred Moten, *The Undercommons: Fugitive Planning & Black Study* (Brooklyn, NY: Autonomedia, 2013).
45. Vishmidt, 'From Speculation to Infrastructure'.
46. Ibid.
47. Saidiya Hartman, 'The Burdened Individuality of Freedom', in *Scenes of Subjection: Terror, Slavery and Self-Making in Nineteenth-Century America* (Oxford: Oxford University Press, 1997).
48. Vishmidt, 'Beneath the Atelier', 227.
49. Vishmidt, 'From Speculation to Infrastructure'.
50. Marina acknowledges her indebtedness to Fred Moten, Denise Ferreira da Silva, Sylvia Wynter, Saidiya Hartman, Hannah Black, David Lloyd and Brenna Bhandar for this turn in her thinking.
51. Vishmidt, 'Only as Self-Relating Negativity', 22. While there isn't adequate space to develop this here, running through much of Marina's work is a critique of the 'ruse of rationality'. In her final years she became interested in the work of Sylvia Wynter and her idea that the human is a 'genre' defined by the overdetermined historical accident of white supremacist patriarchal capitalism. For Marina, the question of what constitutes reason is the very fulcrum of political antagonism.

Total art and mimetic subsumption
Thoughts after Marina Vishmidt
Daniel Spaulding

I knew Marina primarily through her writing, which radiated an intelligence that was sometimes disconcertingly intense. It feels wrong to refer to Marina by her surname, in a way that enforces an academic formality that her voice was constantly occupying and at the same time undermining, in the spirit of Adorno's straining against language to make it crack under the pressure of the dialectic. But since the Marina I know is primarily Marina as she appears in her work, I have the feeling of her being two persons, one textual, one embodied: Marina the comrade and Vishmidt the writer. I know this feeling is incorrect. Still, there's something significant about this (false) split between a writerly and an embodied practice that still has much to give us – in the literal sense that there are unpublished works to look forward to, and in the less literal sense that the larger contours of her thought, its trajectory, and its relevance to struggles both immemorial and yet to come are still emerging. Such 'splitness' also says something about Marina's place amidst and against disciplinarity. In talking about Marina's work, I've sometimes called her an art historian. This is clearly wrong.

The discipline of art history could be understood as a technology for keeping defunct subjectivities on life support, or of revivifying them as hermeneutic zombies. Many of those subjectivities are bourgeois, because the bourgeoisie, for a few centuries, produced, in art, a uniquely dense residue of its ways of being in the world. We have to look at bourgeois paintings – and also of course at aristocratic paintings, courtly statues, peasant pottery, and so on – in ways that the bourgeoisie itself no longer can: maybe, but by no means *certainly*, to preserve an archive of ways of feeling and seeing that don't fit into the present world. And also to keep vivid the fact that even oppression was once different.

Marina's return to moments such as the feminism of the 1970s was the opposite of antiquarian. I think that Marina had little necrophilia in her and accordingly I've never been sure whether the name 'art historian' applies to her, although it would be flattering to the profession if it did. But there is, I'm going to try to argue, a way in which Marina's inquiry rubs at the edges of art history, disclosing thereby a way in which the maddening certainty of a painting like, say, Poussin's *Dance to the Music of Time* at the Wallace Collection – its certainty in conveying something more than a contingent web of signs, but rather a world, in its proper density, in which meaning or ideology (the allegories *as* the passage of time and as real persons at once) inheres as a property of the representational order itself – might dissolve on contact with one or more opposed, untimely totalisations.

For the past few years, I've been trying to rid myself of a book on Joseph Beuys, the German artist who lived from 1921 to 1986 and who invented what he called 'social sculpture' – a kind of art that takes social relations as its material and which accordingly reconceives social forms as themselves 'aesthetic'. This led Beuys to strange propositions, among them, for example, that money ought to be thought of as a collectively shaped 'sculptural' good. Although there are references here and there, so far as I know Marina never discussed Beuys in depth. Nonetheless, as I was returning to *Reproducing Autonomy: Work, Money, Crisis and Contemporary Art*, the book she wrote with Kerstin Stakemeier (published by Mute in 2016), I was struck again by the relevance of Marina's thinking to an interpretation of Beuys that I've been developing for some time.

Beuys' work involves a specific, resonant desire for totalisation that has repeatedly popped up at certain moments in capitalist modernity, probably first with the German Romantics at the end of the eighteenth century. The totalisation is that of art. In effect, social sculpture posits that everything is or can be aesthetic. As Beuys put it, 'Even the act of peeling a potato can be a work of art if it is a conscious act.'[1] Art in this expanded sense becomes indistinguishable from intentional human practice in general.

Photo by Sam Dolbear

What's going on here, clearly, is an expansion of Marcel Duchamp's discovery of the readymade, or the principle that any object can be perceived as a work of art under the proper conditions. Things get tricky in Beuys, though, when this universal aestheticism meets the social or political field. The inference, from which Beuys did not shy away, is that politics or the social must in turn be conceived in plastic terms, as a 'sculpture' of sorts, and thus subject to shaping and reshaping by conscious human will. So far, so good, arguably: this is not incompatible with a classically socialist model of replacing the anarchy of the market with planning. But the analogy gets less comfortable when we ask who exactly plays the role of the sculptor, and what is being sculpted.

Beuys had a few recurring slogans that make things slightly more precise. First, he said that art equals capital. What he meant by this is that creativity ought to be the basic driving and mediating force in the coming order that he called 'free democratic socialism', as capital is in our present world. Your ability to create (in the expanded sense in which peeling a potato is a creative act, too) is your capital. Second, he claimed that everyone is an artist. Creativity is not confined to a specific social role or class or profession but is rather innate in everyone. But what happens to those two theses when we add them up? If everyone is an artist, and art equals capital, then everyone is a capitalist, too. What we have now is not 'free democratic socialism' so much as the world that Marina wrote about so effectively in her 2018 book *Speculation as a Mode of Production*: the world of so-called human capital, in which art comes to model universalised entrepreneurial subjectivity. What's happened, then, is that a Duchampian totalisation of art has turned out not to result in the romanticisation of the world, as Novalis imagined in 1798, but rather art's mimesis of capital. This is a terminus that paradoxically seems to dissolve aesthetic autonomy in universalising it.

What's involved here is a two-way mimesis, though. In *Reproducing Autonomy*, Marina briefly describes post-Duchampian art in terms of what she calls 'mimetic subsumption'. Subsumption notoriously has two varieties, formal and real. The readymade, or the 'nominalist gesture' of selecting something as an artwork, is a machine that recruits potentially anything to the status of art, as capital can subsume many things. But of course, art in modernity is also in an important and perhaps definitional way exceptional with respect to standard commodity production.[2] The exchange-value of artworks is not generally regulated by socially necessary labour time, although artworks enter into more general exchange relations. Art is indirectly market-mediated. This is the basis on which Marina correlates art with social reproduction, to which the domain of aesthetic semblance would at first seem not to be very close. And this issue of semblance or its absence will be important.

So, there are two dynamics of totalisation in play here: that of capital and that of art, neither of which, in principle, possesses an absolute limit. Art's mimetic subsumption of anything meets and mirrors, but is not identical with, capital's subsumption of production processes. The latter, for one thing, doesn't obviously involve mimesis. Yet what Marina seems to be suggesting here is precisely that it does: capital relates to its indirectly mediated reproductive sphere as Duchamp relates to a urinal.

Now, let's step back and observe that the readymade model was in its time a displacement of a prior matrix of artistic subsumption. In the long period between Giotto and Manet, approximately, in other words from the early fourteenth to the mid-nineteenth centuries, European painting conjured phenomenological spaces that possess a certain finality. Poussin's *Dance to the Music of Time* is here my synecdoche for everything that this tradition contains. I'm inclined to attach the phrase 'the age of the picture-world' to this unit of history, in contrast to Heidegger's 'age of the world-picture'.

The age of the picture-world can be defined as that phase of Western culture during which images on a two-dimensional surface can claim to correspond to a total sense of embodied reality. It would be easy to reduce this totalising claim to ocularcentrism, or to the identification of vision as such with immobile single-point perspective. But rigorous perspectival constructions are an inessential aspect of the picture-world. More important is that a conviction be conveyed to the viewer that a represented space is continuous, contains bodies – whether of human beings, still life objects, landscape features, etc. – and is complete, meaning that there are neither parts of the pictorial field that are unaccountable in terms of the totalised reality effect, nor ontological disruptions that negate the continuity of space and bodies. This sort of picture-world can undoubtedly contain supernatural entities and events. It can show rupture and paradox. But it makes those discrepancies part of its continuity. Time plays a lyre. Apollo floats in the sky. Time and Apollo are *real*.

This subsumption of space and bodies to a totalised pictorial field precedes and parallels capital's subsumption of things to the value-form, but is also incommensurate with the social synthesis accomplished by real abstraction, which reduces phenomenal qualitative equivalence to abstract quantitative equivalence.[3] The picture-world probably ends with the rise of what Guy Debord called spectacle. Everyone who knows a little about modern art will have her own candidates, but as I see it, the last instances of picture-world painting can be found in Cubism – including examples as attenuated as Braque's late studios – and in Matisse and Bonnard, and maybe some Jackson Pollocks that are more like landscapes. The recovery of something resembling a picture-world also seems to be a recurrent if usually frustrated aspect of the past century's art. Nicole Eisenman has been trying it out, for example.

Photo by Sam Dolbear

The point is that there was and perhaps in a tenuous way still is a cultural realm in which picture-world and readymade coexist as shapes of totalisation within and occasionally against the wrong totality of capital. Much of the story of modern art can be told as that of the migration of semblance from residual bourgeois representational technologies to specifically capitalist forms of appearance. (Technical reproducibility – the paradigmatic analysis of which remains, of course, Walter Benjamin's famous essay – has long been the chief means with which to achieve the real subsumption of semblance and thus, arguably, its ruin.[4]) The readymade is a moment in which mimesis shrinks to the mere fact that an object imitates itself, which differentiates a thing thus designated from a formally identical thing not thus designated. But the way in which these two artistic modalities – readymade and picture-world – subsumed things always lagged a step behind capital. Representation alters what it rep-

Photo by Sam Dolbear

resents, and an object that turns into a readymade is different from what it was before. Nonetheless, pictorial representation as well as the readymade both take their objects as given – as empirical forms that dictate their aesthetic analogies. They both have a reality principle, in other words. Politics, too, can sometimes intrude as a massiveness that even artists can't avoid. Something like this happened in France after the revolution of 1848, or in Berlin Dada's refraction of the Spartakus revolt. A reality principle need not generate realism in its familiar meaning.

Things dictate art, but art also seizes things without wholly abrogating their autonomy. Although the analogy is deliberately tenuous, I want to call the latter process 'mimetic formal subsumption', in order to compare it with capital's formal subsumption of production processes on which it does not yet impose a substantially new organisation. A readymade remains the same thing;

its relations have simply been reordered. A picture-world still has to be a world.

What, then, would be the aesthetic counterpart to *real* subsumption – subsumption that alters production and labour in its image? And what specifically aesthetic logic might correspond to specifically capitalist rationality? Maybe none; it may be that art simply doesn't do this, at least as long as semblance is in play – which may be a reason not to assent at once to an abstract negation of the aesthetic. This would take us to Adorno and other disagreeable subjects. I'm going to have to bracket both this and the many debates over real versus formal subsumption in Marxist theory. I should at least clarify that I don't believe that either term names a historical period. Still, the labour of representation involves techniques, and if mimetic real subsumption exists it probably involves a closer dialogue with general social technique than do the reserved archaic technologies of paint and brush. There needs to be a medium.

Cameron Rowland is an artist Marina wrote about at some length, for instance in a review of an exhibition of his at the Institute of Contemporary Art, London, in 2020. The mahogany doors of the ICA were produced by enslaved labour and, all else being equal, would continue to accrue value to their owners, namely the British royal family. For his show, Rowland set up a corporation to which the ICA mortgaged the doors as well as a mahogany handrail inside the building. He also stipulated that the mortgage would not be repaid – an arrangement that constitutes what is known as an encumbrance on any future transaction. This lowers the value of the property and by extension the British crown's net worth, with no physical alteration.

'Art' and 'value' seize hold of the same object. But 'art' acts here as a mimetic subsumption of property law, which becomes – unusually – a weapon *against* value. Law remains unaltered. Mimetic subsumption is perhaps inherently unreal when applied to genuinely effective forms. The best it can do is to use law as a medium with which to injure another social form. And nobody has claimed that paintings can abolish paint. Arguably, one thing the perspective of infrastructural critique does is to shift the site of medium to a substrate that obligates a different notion of practice – practice that would by its nature exceed the aesthetic.

But the aesthetic turns out not to be so easy to uproot. As Marina put it, 'Here, the legal instrument of encumbrance becomes akin to a termite colony – commodity fetishism riddled with subterranean channels. The inescapable ownership relation between the ICA and the Crown Estate gets aerated by this parasitical one, which the institution has itself invited, sanctioned and signed.'[5] Or, as she states a little later in the same article: 'In its many-sided thoroughness, Rowland's practice puts one in mind of a crystal drill, if there is such a device: It creates sight lines by cutting through language, provenances, and histories, but the cutting apparatus is already a prism.'[6]

Termites with prismatic crystal drills: one feels Marina grasping here for a set of metaphors that would irradiate the incision of transformative practice with the shine of semblance, down through history, through infrastructure, through 'our busy insect-like comings and goings', to quote Monsieur Dupont.[7] This is art history as it might be when the kaleidoscope turns.

Notes

1. Willoughby Sharp, 'An Interview with Joseph Beuys', *Artforum* 8:4 (December 1969), 40–47.
2. As Dave Beech has most exhaustively demonstrated. See Dave Beech, *Art and Value: Art's Economic Exceptionalism in Classical, Neoclassical, and Marxist Economics* (Leiden and Boston: Brill, 2015).
3. Alfred Sohn-Rethel develops the notions of real abstraction and social synthesis in his book *Intellectual and Manual Labour: A Critique of Epistemology*, trans. Martin Sohn-Rethel (Leiden and Boston: Brill, 2021).
4. Walter Benjamin, 'The Work of Art in the Age of Its Technological Reproducibility', trans. Edmond Jephcott and Harry Zohn, in *Selected Writings, Volume 3: 1935–1938*, eds. Howard Eiland and Michael W. Jennings (Cambridge, MA: Harvard University Press, 2002).
5. Marina Vishmidt, 'Cameron Rowland', *Artforum* 58:8 (April 2020), 164.
6. Vishmidt, 'Cameron Rowland', 165.
7. Monsieur Dupont, *Nihilist Communism: A Critique of Optimism (the Religious Dogma that States There Will Be an Ultimate Triumph of Good Over Evil) in the Far Left* (Cambridge: Monsieur Dupont, 2003), 1.

Minor compositions
Marina Vishmidt's collaborations
E.C. Feiss

The spate of short essays published since Marina Vishmidt's passing have endeavoured to catalogue her major works: to summarise the immense, multifaceted contribution, only beginning to be digested, of her book *Speculation as a Mode of Production*, and to map the parameters of her theory of 'infrastructural critique' before the phrase is aerosolised in the ether of the art and academic milieu in which she trafficked, separated from the precision and utility embedded in her original articulation of the concept. As many have noted, Marina often shunned the standard markers of intellectual property common to the academic and art institutionalisation of thought in favour of a million partnerships, some easy to point to and others less so. Consider the countless exercises frequent within her life practice – informal crits, reading groups, summer camps, partnership with various small art institutions or formations, and heterogenous forms of organizing -- a grind as immaterial to her published record now as it is baked into how certain art worlds – between the UK, the EU and increasingly the U.S. – understand their bind with capital. Her fleshly, lifelong commitment to an intellectual commons was grounded in how she worked every day; it was equally philosophical and methodological. This latter point is especially important given that, in my view, there is a mundane gendered reason for the fact that although Marina's work shaped a particular art world configuration for the last decade, she has not been exalted to the extent of her male art theorist peers, even if she had begun more recently to receive the kind of institutional recognition her work demanded. This lag stems too from the way she operated, with an eye to the living ground of thought, to its genesis in common. Thus, a shorthand has developed to account for the numerous set-ups this commons took – that she was a writer, professor, mentor, organiser, critic, editor, programmer, etc, alongside and as fuel to her theoretical production. What I want to address, with inevitable inadequacy, are some points of integral feedback between this praxis and her theoretical production.

The generative quality of this exchange can be understood under the awning of 'criticism', as she unraveled that term and as it traversed her academic, art institutional and organisational activity. In other words, I'm going to address Marina's impact on art. Surely art and its world(s) was the 'convenience store', as Kerstin Stakemeier recently put it, of her archive, a stop on the side of the road in her pursuit of articulating the terms of unfreedom and the possible paths of its contestation.[1] Yet art and its determinate contexts, which she catalogued casually, and with a singular precision, were frequent infrastructures, social and material, offering a certain autonomy of means for her writing. I am thinking here most immediately of the appearance of her thought in many smaller formats outside the larger book projects, as well as the discursive production that filled many an EU-funded cultural space. Another example would be the many – particularly female – writers, like myself, who Marina fortified, whose collective output has slowly integrated into art theory and criticism, how it's done, and what we expect it to do.[2] The impact of Marina's work in this sense isn't measurable, or perhaps might only be decades from now. Or we could insist that the immeasurability of all this 'minor' production is a feature of its structural relation to the world it created. As Marina summarised this recently:

> the constitutive exception, whether it is reproductive labour in the home or the unquantifiable reproductive labour of the cultural worker or the serviceable artist: the 'under-labourer' who is the condition of possibility of the system's ability to reproduce itself as a whole, the 'work' that must disappear in order for 'the work' to appear, whether that work is the waged worker or the art installation.[3]

Marina Vishmidt at We are the Time Machines: Time and Tools for Commoning (WTM), Forum IV: Commoning Aesthetics, 12 March 2016, 14:00–18:00 at Casco HQ. Photo by Cee Bakker. Courtesy: Casco Art Institute: Working for the Commons.

As many have noted, Marina practiced what she theorised; this also entailed that her own 'under-labour', namely all the activity, from small format writing to organising, outside of her central oeuvre, fashioned the art system she circulated in. Provisionally, we can trace this in three guises. First, the historical effects propelled by her thought, trackable through institutional, and counter institutional, formations. Second, how Marina's criticism enacted the kind of partnerships she forged in the rest of her life, writing with and alongside works of art in pursuit of more exacting social theory rather than as part of (or sometimes self-consciously pointing to) the processes of valorisation her work tracked at large. Finally, the way that – at a remove from art history and aesthetic theory – Marina's writing renovated the artistic subject through capturing the terms of its relationship to the 'automatic subject' of capital, nullifying the possibility of perceiving this artistic subject in singular terms, despite the near complete disciplinary mandate to do so; how the automatic subject of self-valorising value 'shapes the activity of the practitioner', or in other words, how social form in capital preconditions what the artist can begin to think, much less produce, changes the terms of writing – description, the question of assessment – on artworks. [4]

Marina was a key critical theorist of art after the 2008 financial crisis, who responded to but also expanded post-operaist theories of artistic labour by integrating theories of social reproduction. Social reproduction theory wasn't an applied analytic but how she configured her overall practice, in the creation of the artistic realities she wrote about. There are the numerous artists organisations she shaped and was shaped by, perhaps most pertinently to what I'm arguing here is W.A.G.E. (Working Artists and the Greater Economy) which has reconfigured consciousness around artists' labour and its institutional conditions, and arguably had a hand in the frameworks available to the last decade of museum strikes (such as the New Museum in 2019 and Tate United in 2020).[5] As much as she would reject the attribution of any singular influence, including her own, on a mass mobilization, or shift in labour consciousness, of cultural workers, she's not here to argue with me. The urgency of her intervention in these earlier years lay in the excavation of what happens after the popular recognition of art as work and what this entailed for theory, and particularly for organising around the determination of their interlinked value. It was inseparable from her own involvement in these emergent struggles that her criticism shaped how a contingent of artists understood the form, location and function of their labour in the greater economy, so to speak.

Marina's earliest stewardship of this subject – editing the volume *Immaterial Labour: Work, Research, and Art* (2003) and her writing for *Mute*, particularly the essay 'Precarious Straits' (2005), on issues resulting from the equation of art with precarious labour – predates the founding of W.A.G.E in 2008.[6] Her seminal essay 'Situation Wanted: Something about Labour', condensing and departing from the mounting literature on art and labour, appeared in *Afterall* in 2008, the year of the crisis.[7] She would be the first to say that many others also drew new linkages between art, labour and value in the fury surrounding the financial collapse. Indeed, the *Immaterial Labour* volume was a collaboration with Melanie Gilligan who would become a regular co-author over the course of the next decade. However, Marina's articulation of how art is a 'specialised niche' within the dynamic of real subsumption had a particular saliency, because it assessed the poles of art and value beyond the framework of the commodity and provided a necessary counterpoint to the limited organisational imagination for an artist's wage. Essays like 'Mimesis of the Hardened and Alienated: Social Practice as Business Model' (2013) narrated how art's logic of 'disruptive innovation', a process within capital's unabating incorporation of all that lies outside of it, explained not only the baldly 'threadbare and transparent' procedure of arts-led gentrification but the production of life-forms and activities shared between the vanguard outer lip (as one and the same threshold) of contemporary art practices and the technics of accumulation. In this essay, that was the entrepreneurial figure stationed at the heart of the surge in artist's social practice, 'distinguished by a pragmatism that appears subversive at first glance', against which she furnished a genealogy of that self-motivated character stretching from DIY 'small ownership' culture in the Thatcher era through to NGOs and micro-finance.[8] In turn, she consulted for W.A.G.E on policy regarding 'the value of non-monetary compensation' for artists, as well as the contract mechanism for deciding which activities are tied to the artists' fee, beyond the delivery of the discrete art object.[9] She also relentlessly criticized the organisation, in many a board meeting or strategy summit, for its role in the socialization of art as abstract labour even as she pragmatically aided it at every turn. Her work thought with and in excess of the expected categories of artists' involvement in the economy – the question of the wage and the figure of the commodity. Instead, in demonstrating how contemporary art uniquely facilitates capital's evolving vanguard, she also located logics of solidarity for artists with those who labour on the non-valorised side of the reproductive border, particularly underpaid domestic workers such as those represented by groups like Italy's Chainworkers and San Precario Union and the National Domestic Workers Alliance in the U.S., founded in 2007.[10]

In true dialectical fashion, she wrote about consultants while serving as a clandestine one herself, critically informing several key feminist public art spaces as a board member and general touchstone, as funding for these types of institutions began to dwindle in the UK and EU.[11] Organisations like CASCO in Utrecht and the Showroom in London developed exhibitions on reproduction (as a body of theory and as a social reality in art histories) in consultation with her long before the art system's hazy discourse on 'care' appeared post-COVID.[12] How an analysis of reproduction – as undergirding value – has reconfigured art's politics cannot be overstated.[13] It renovated the subject of the artist-worker, the sites and forms of what counts as her work, particularly the border between the art object and the life processes understood to be included in its production, and therefore the terms of both exchange and confrontation between artist and institution. Marina's work both cut through a masculinist art theory Left, caught in the intractable embrace of a Situationist-derived tactical imagination, and illuminated other histories that this version of an artist-subject-revolution couldn't apprehend. What does it mean that social reproduction theory and the history of Wages for Housework have broadly been art institutionalised? One measure is Silvia Federici's appearance in both Documenta 13 (2012) and 15 (2022).[14] What does that incorporation, which I am inferring was partly facilitated by Marina's thought, entail for what she called the 'value-form of artistic subjectivity', or in other words, what politics does it enable and what kind of foreclosure – what kind of institutional guardrails and preconceptions of activity or possibility – does it introduce to the materialist feminism it also invokes? We need Marina now to point towards how we, those still allied with art as a potentially pliable corner of financialised capitalism, 'win an autonomy with a general, socialized horizon.'[15] Or in other words, how we pursue the extension of art's autonomy to its fullest imaginable realisation, 'to effect a more thoroughgoing transformation of social life and productive relations, one that would render autonomy specifically for art or culture redundant.'[16]

Photo by Cee Bakker. Courtesy: Casco Art Institute: Working for the Commons.

Marina's writing on and with art disenabled the embattled but still very much alive project of modernist criticism – to demarcate, to valorise – kept on life support by writing that furnishes the artwork with untold humanistic capacities, sustained by the laissez faire procedure of, as one example, the many critics who continue to write for *Artforum* despite the boycott of it in solidarity with Gaza. That the critical authority of art rests on a platform invested in genocide (perhaps an inevitability given the colonial underpinnings of aesthetic judgement) situates one such iteration, one narrative, of Marina's departure from 'criticism'. Instead, she utilised art within a larger project on the relations of value today, producing a form of writing about art that sought the demise of it and its present conditions; a seamstress of the negative if there ever was one. What kind of value, then, did her writing in the field of art generate, if we think about 'criticism' as normatively directly productive of art's stature? Her work produced social, historical and specifically labour consciousness for artists; it also imagined tactical and organisational schema, and it functioned like the traditional broadside, albeit in a materialist lyrical form, to diagnose and build collective feeling toward action.

In 2009 for example she wrote of works by Melanie Gilligan ('Crisis in the Credit System') and Blaise Kirschner, artists with whom she would remain close, about how the 'opacity and argument' of their work deflected a reactionary curatorial melancholia around the crisis for the cultural sector created by the larger financial meltdown.[17] Writing on Rosa Barba's exhibition at the Turner Contemporary in Margate, Marina read the artist's employment of film as a device of inherent repetition, as an 'engine' of production rather than a medium, through the work's inevitable participation in the culture-led regeneration of that city. What that reading entails for Barba's position is left relatively ambiguous, but perhaps resonant in the way her antique, 'tender devices break down easily', interrupting the unimpeded drive of the institution through their fragile form.[18] She showed us how both Cameron Rowland and Grace Schwindt, two artists who at first seem unalike, grasp that 'medium-specificity has changed by now, now that the medium includes the market.'[19] The phrasing links Rowland's manipulation of the real legal instruments of racialised property and Schwindt's furnishing of liberalism's embodied voice, to build the terms of an artistic posture between institution, artwork and market based on a relation rather than the standard markers of comparison (style, material, method).[20] Rather than a method, Marina identifies an artistic orientation to the space between the art object, its space of appearance and the market, in any given circumstance with any specified tools. In one of her last published art writings, an exchange with Claire Fontaine, she asked broad questions of their recent involvement in the Venice Biennale (2024), the reception of which is now cluttered with misguided treatises on the supposed dominance of 'identity' in contemporary art. Instead, Marina asked if their work 'sharpens antagonism' or 'provides resources' against the rise of a xenophobic far right (including Giorgia Meloni's government in Italy) beyond the inevitable limits of the exhibition's cosmopolitanism. She used the situation of their practice to pose, not the problematic of 'identity' within the confines of an updated multiculturalism, but the potential of a "human strike" against the increasingly unlivable present.[21]

Marina's materialist criticism also manifested through her lucid descriptions of the exhibition's surrounds, placing artist and artwork in a wide and richly realised landscape. For example, she writes of the quality of the stone inlaid around the Turner Contemporary against the duller asphalt and iron otherwise used on walkways in Margate. She contrasts the lush curtains in Marres Contemporary Art Centre with the uncertainty of its institutional coffers. This is one way she lined the passage between art's exception in capitalism and how that exception concretely appears in the social field. There are the artworks in question amid a set of curatorial decisions, but there are also all the tangible realities surrounding art in its realised state which exceed how the exhibition self-determines: the city it's in and the coarse history of its present, the interior designer, administrators and city planners who furnished, organised and sign-posted the institution. Such details are one means by which Marina's criticism refused to attribute any sense of singular agency to artist or artwork outside of their determination within the present relations of production and history. This is how she isolated what actual 'determinate negations', artistic gestures able to evince contradiction within capital, could achieve vis a vis an artwork's contingent space of exception, a practical autonomy she hemmed tightly to the presiding details of possibility (whether the specificities of the institution or the discourse of 'creativity').[22]

Most writing on art, whether variants of art history, criticism or aesthetic theory, contains an artist subject whose criticality manages to transcend even the dutiful plotting of his complicity within the immediate frame. It is worth briefly noting that where art history and its ancillaries can be easily dismissed, with the discipline's evident roots in connoisseurship, the presumptive subject of aesthetic theory in the German tradition – ratified in Adorno's thought, which *Speculation* departs from – is also one constitutively separated from labour, occupying an autonomous sphere from which it produces under alternate terms. Marina's writing frayed this configuration by showing how contemporary capitalism rendered all labour 'creative', seemingly incorporeal, and future leveraged, while also showing how, like the illusory but intractable realm of art's state of exception, the value of speculative capital (in art or finance) is dependent on concrete labour. The level of abstraction she wielded in her writings served to place a fuller range of aesthetic subjects, including but not limited to artists, within the spectrum of analysis. One important aspect of this is how, with an indifferent negativity, it displaces the artist from the centre of aesthetic inquiry without removing her entirely. Her range of subjects includes the familiar homology between artist and entrepreneur, but also those at work in the inverted shadow of speculative production, such as those on right-to-work rolls, miming work to receive a welfare check.[23]

Marina Vishmidt at Policy People 1, organised by E. C. Feiss and Karisa Senavitis, W139 Gallery, March 28, 2015. Photos Kym Ward.

I attempted to use Marina's rendering of speculative value – that it describes art's elastic appreciation as well as indebtedness or wagelessness – to describe a set of relationships (in 1961, at an earlier onset point of post-

Fordism) between an artist, his sculpture and the lumpenproletariat around him. I don't think he consciously perceived the relation between his art and the surrounding unwaged population. Instead, I argue that this uneven economic landscape produced both him and his art, if not the sculpture's intimate formal elements, but certainly its available materials and the basis of its display. For example, his performance – as a "shopkeeper" in a gallery-cum-bodega – was isomorphic, to use a Marina word, with the kinds of welfare job play (as fake cashiers, gas attendants and servers in state-run establishments) these unemployed people were mandated to do. The art history journal that ultimately published it converted most of the argument into one where the artist maintained his interiority, if largely through a lapse to shared historical 'context.' The reviewers kept saying I had a subject-object problem – what was I arguing the artist was doing? Perhaps it was my own clumsy application, but this reception indicates how artistic authorship remains largely unassailable, fully insulated by its exceptional status. A more recent essay in the same journal uses Marina's work to argue that a certain artist 'speculates' or 'speculated', ironically collapsing an argument about class stratification into a descriptor of artistic innovation, but I imagine that was also a disciplinary conversion made through the pasta strainer of the review board. The focus in her writing ultimately never fell primarily on the artist's gesture, but rather on how an oblique view of it furnished a model for understanding contemporary modes of extraction as well as the 'speculative and creative dimensions of antagonism.'[24] This is why criticism of *Speculation* for its lack of examples in artistic practice is banal and misguided – such case studies simply need collection from across her wider corpus, but art is also not really the point. I wonder whether, in some particularly heady corners of the later work, she began to offer 'examples' only through her graphic prose rather than external art objects.

Widespread mourning for her passing feels weighted, as Sven Lütticken recently put it, by the compounding of the loss with the deterioration of the Left's power more broadly.[25] The loss of Marina though is more specific to her role within that enfeebled Left, or, to put it another way, we feel the chasm of her departure at an increasingly frightening time. We lose her role as a narrator of and guide to our conditions; the loss of her abruptly terminates, as she and Melissa Gordon once put it, the building of the collective 'we' that she wove so carefully with others.[26]

Thanks to Danny Hayward, Kerstin Stakemeier and Avigail Moss

Notes

1. Kerstin Stakemeier, 'Marina's Cues', *eflux notes*, May 31 2024, https://www.e-flux.com/notes/611821/marina-s-cues.
2. Larne Abse-Gogarty expresses a similar sentiment in her obituary: 'Marina Vishmidt 1976-2024', *Art Monthly* 477 (June 2024): 24.
3. Marina Vishmidt, 'The Aesthetic Subject and the Politics of Speculative Labour', in *The Routledge Companion to Art and Politics*, ed. Randy Martin (London: Routledge, 2015), 30.
4. Marina Vishmidt, *Speculation as a Mode of Production* (Leiden: Brill, 2018), 6.
5. The dialectical relationship between Marina's thought and organising is beautifully catalogued in the obituary that precedes the archive of her work: https://on-vishmidt.memoryoftheworld.org/marina-vishmidt/.
6. Marina Vishmidt, and Melanie Gilligan, eds., *Immaterial Labour: Work, Research and Art. De- Dis- Ex Volume 5* (London: Black Dog Press, 2004); Marina Vishmidt, 'Precarious Straits', *Mute*, August 2, 2005, https://www.metamute.org/editorial/articles/precarious-straits.
7. Marina Vishmidt, 'Situation Wanted: Something about Labour', *Afterall: A Journal of Art, Context and Enquiry* 19 (October 2008), 20–34.
8. Marina Vishmidt, '"Mimesis of the Hardened and Alienated": Social Practice as Business Model', *eflux journal* 43 (March 2013), http://www.e-flux.com/journal/43/60197/mimesis-of-the-hardened-and-alienated-social-practice-as-business-model/.
9. 'W.A.G.E. Certification Development Materials', W.A.G.E., https://wageforwork.com/certificationdevelopmentmaterials#top.
10. Marina writes about the Chainworkers and San Precario in 'Precarious Straits'.
11. Other organisations included the Centre for Contemporary Art, Derry, CuratorLab, Konsfack, Stockholm, Marabouparken and Konsthall C, Stockholm, Arthur Boskamp-Stiftung/M.1, Hohenlockstedt, Germany.
12. *The Grand Domestic Revolution – User's Manual* (2009-2012), Casco – Office for Art, Design and Theory, Utrecht. Marina gave a the seminar for the Dutch Art Institute (Arnhem, NL) in the context of *User's Manual: The Grand*

Domestic Revolution on Feb 18, 2010. She published the essay 'Self-Negating Labour: A Spasmodic Chronology of Domestic Unwork' in Binna Choi and Maiko Tanaka, eds., *The Grand Domestic Revolution Goes on* (London; Utrecht: Bedford Press, Casco, 2010), 53–90.

13. Much of this theory was also co-written with Kerstin Stakemeier and Zoe Sutherland.

14. For example Documenta 13 (2012) published Silvia Federici's *Witch-Hunting, Past and Present, and the Fear of the Power of Women* as part of its 100 Notes-100 Thoughts publication series. Federici's work was included in the Commoning Curatorial and Artistic Education series in Documenta 15 (2022), see: https://documenta-fifteen.de/en/calendar/commoning-curatorial-and-artistic-education-7/. On this issue (of the discourse of the commons and issues of social reproduction in the institution of art), see Marina Vishmidt, 'All Shall Be Unicorns', *Open*, September 3, 2014, https://www.onlineopen.org/all-shall-be-unicorns and especially, Vishmidt, The Manifestation of the Discourse of the Commons in the Field of Art, KUNCI Study Forum and Collective, March 3, 2015, https://www.kunci.or.id/ulasan/marina-vishmidt-commons-in-the-field-of-art/.

15. Kerstin Stakemeier and Marina Vishmidt, *Reproducing Autonomy: Work, Money, Crisis and Contemporary Art* (London Berlin: Mute, 2016), 67–68.

16. Marina Vishmidt and Sven Lütticken, 'Genealogies of Autonomy', *eflux* 149 (November 2024), https://www.e-flux.com/journal/149/637373/genealogies-of-autonomy/.

17. Marina Vishmidt, 'I'M TOO SAD TO SELL YOU. On "The Avantgarde: Depression" at Marres Centre for Contemporary Culture, Maastricht', *Texte zur Kunst* online, December 3, 2009, https://www.textezurkunst.de/en/articles/im-too-sad-sell-you-depression-marres-centre-conte/. For more of Marina's writing on Blaise Kirschner, see '"Lights, Camera, Now-Time! Polly II: Plan for a Revolution in Docklands": Marina Vishmidt on a New Film by Anja Kirschner* (*Blaise Kirschner)', *Mousse Magazine*, October 7 2024, https://www.moussemagazine.it/magazine/marina-vishmidt-kerstin-stakemeier-danny-hayward-blaise-kirschner 2024.

18. Marina Vishmidt, 'A Rapid Inventory of the Universe: Marina Vishmidt on Rosa Barba at Turner Contemporary, Margate', *Texte zur Kunst* 90 (June 2013), https://www.textezurkunst.de/en/90/vishmidt-barba-rapid-inventory-universe/.

19. Marina Vishmidt, 'Fragile Prop in Constant Danger: On Some Motifs in Grace Schwindt's Works', in *Run a Home, Build a Town, Lead a Revolution. An Exhibition in Three Acts*, ed. Agar Ledo (Vigo: Fundación MARCO, 2017).

20. Vishmidt, 'Fragile Prop'; Vishmidt, 'On Cameron Rowland', *Artforum* 58:8 (April, 2020), 164–65.

21. Marina Vishmidt and Claire Fontaine, 'We Can Refuse to Abdicate in a Number of Ways', *Mousse Magazine*, April 3 2024, https://www.moussemagazine.it/magazine/claire-fontaine-marina-vishmidt-2024

22. The concept of determinate negation, from Adorno's *Negative Dialectics*, is one Marina frequently employed. For the 'creative subject', see Vishmidt, 'Precarious Straits' and Vishmidt, *Speculation*.

23. Vishmidt, *Speculation*, 10–11.

24. Marina Vishmidt and Andreas Petrossiants, 'Spaces of Speculation: Movement Politics in the Infrastructure', *Historical Materialism* (blog), November 14, 2020, https://www.historicalmaterialism.org/spaces-of-speculation-movement-politics-in-the-infrastructure/.

25. Sven Lutticken, 'Memories of Marina – Marina Vishmidt, 1976-2024', *Institute of Network Cultures*, https://networkcultures.org/blog/2024/05/03/memories-of-marina-marina-vishmidt-1976-2024/.

26. 'We not I' was a programme Gordon and Vishmidt ran between 2014-2015 and in which I participated along with many others. A related conversation between the two was published as 'From I to We', conversation with Melissa Gordon and editors, in *Politics of Study*, eds. Sidsel Meineche Hansen and Tom Vandeputte (London and Odense: Open Editions and Funen Art Academy, 2015), 103–112.

Reviews

Aporetic Marxism

Gillian Rose, *Marxist Modernism: Introductory Lectures on the Frankfurt School and Critical Theory* (London: Verso, 2024). 176pp., £17.99 pb., 978 1 80429 011 8

'You've probably heard of sexual fetishism, but not commodity fetishism!', quips Gillian Rose in the first of her 1979 lectures on the Frankfurt School at the University of Sussex. A few scattered titters ring out in the scratchy recording. Transcribed and reprinted with a forward by editors James Gordon Finlayson and Robert Lukas Scott, and an afterward by Martin Jay, *Marxist Modernism: Introductory Lectures on the Frankfurt School and Critical Theory* is a collection of lectures given early in Rose's career aiming to introduce the Frankfurt School to undergraduate students and intervene in the debate on Marxism and aesthetics. Read within her broader oeuvre, *Marxist Modernism* is also a fascinating document when tracing out the stakes of the eventual fierce debate on Rose's relationship to Marxist thought. In these lectures and her broader work, Rose enacts a hybrid reading of a variety of Marxist modernisms – especially through her entanglement with Adorno – that asks what constitutes the category of critical Marxism.

Rose's early work was grounded in the Frankfurt School. Her first book, a reworked version of her doctoral dissertation, *The Melancholy Science: An Introduction to the Work of Theodor Adorno*, was published in 1978. Commentators on Rose's work often debate whether she shifted away from Marxist thought after her subsequent *Hegel Contra Sociology* (1981) in which she seems to break with Adorno's negative dialectics, before later presenting her own speculative dialectics in *The Broken Middle: Out of Our Ancient Society* (1992).

Rose's speculative dialectics is based on a reading of Hegel in which the unresolved space of mediation between two positions is privileged over synthesis. It is thus not a teleological progression towards a Hegelian absolute endpoint, but posits the absolute as a speculative, unfolding process of mediation. Rose termed this space 'the broken middle', or the constant mediation of individual and state, grace and law, immanent and transcendent. Throughout her work, the broken middle figures as the fuel for political engagement of citizens within the modern state. Grounded in her critique of postmodernism's lack of ethical claims and scepticism of a crudely economist Marxism, the broken middle is also a site in which Christian theology entered Rose's thought. This occurs through her fraught attempts to bring a Hegelian structure in conversation with Kierkegaard's idea of a 'leap of faith', utilised to conceptualise the act of committing to God or any absolute truth. Christian and Jewish theological themes appear in her later *Mourning Becomes the Law: Philosophy and Representation*, *Judaism and Modernity: Philosophical Essays*, and her philosophical memoir for which she achieved popular fame before her untimely death in 1995 at the age of 48, *Love's Work*.

In his 1982 review of *Hegel contra Sociology*, notably the first article he authored for *Radical Philosophy*, former Rose student Peters Osborne set the conversation for future debates on Rose's legacy. In it, he discusses Rose's attempt to re-orient critical theory back to Hegel, captured by her neologism 'critical Marxism'. This means 'the exposition of capitalism as culture', 'a presentation of the contradictory relations between Capital and culture' in the phenomeno-logical (speculative) mode.' It is rooted in Rose's argument that Marx's practical materialistic critique of Hegel was inadequate, because it was theoretically unable to understand abstract dichotomies between theory and practice, being and consciousness. Osborne sees this reading as an attempt to reformulate the concept of Critical Theory, with broader implications for Marxist thought. Yet in his 2015 article 'Gillian Rose and Marxism', also published in *Radical Philosophy*, Osborne writes that

> In the light of her subsequent writings, the project of a critical Marxism appears as a conjuncturally overdetermined first draft for the much more general project of (re)thinking the political potential of the European philosophical tradition – principally, German idealism

and its aftermath – which, while it emerged out of Rose's reading of Adorno, always involved, via the absolutist element of its constructively eccentric Hegelianism, a certain theological aspect or inflection.

Ultimately arguing that the term critical Marxism itself is irrelevant in a post-1989 Marxist climate, Osborne points to Adorno's *Aesthetic Theory* as a source of inspiration and asks if 'perhaps there is an opportunity here to think out of a different kind of broken middle'. *Marxist Modernism* provides such an opportunity by illuminating the gaps between Rose's and Adorno's speculative and fixed concepts, critique and material politics.

In the late seventies Rose was working as a reader at Sussex, teaching in 'The Modern European Mind', a course for third-year undergraduates centred on the confluence of Marx, Freud and Nietzsche. As Martin Jay notes in his afterword, Rose's focus on Marxism, modernism and aesthetics was state-of-the-art in the UK at that moment, following in the footsteps of Fredric Jameson's *Marxism and Form* (1971) and anticipating Eugene Lunn's *Marxism and Modernism* (1984). In the lectures that make up *Marxist Modernism*, Rose is keen to present an image of an ununified modernism made up of competing literary and artistic movements that parallel the disagreements between Frankfurt School figures and adjacent thinkers, moving from Lukács to Bloch, Benjamin, Horkheimer and Adorno, and Brecht back to Adorno.

This understanding of modernisms supplements her other overarching point that the main move of critical theory was to generalise and radicalise Marx's understanding of commodity fetishism via Lukács's concept of reification introduced in *History and Class Consciousness* (1923). Rose discusses how most associates of the Frankfurt School embraced this term to critique and extend Marxism, approaching the issue of domination beyond a mere economic and political lens and extending it into art, music and literature. Various modernist movements, ranging from Dada to Surrealism to Expressionism, were embedded in the possibilities of culture both as a tool of domination and a means of resistance to it.

In Rose's exposition Lukács receives the harshest critique for the dogmatic works authoured late in his career, containing his attempts to differentiate between decadent modernism and emancipatory socialist realism. *Modernisms* here signals a dialectical movement in which critique emerges from various opinions and their discontents. Her main critique of Marx is that he did not properly consider culture; her main critique of the Frankfurt School thinkers is that they fail to consider the dynamic movement within terms such as emancipation, revolution and technology. Roses critiques Bloch for placing too much emancipatory potential in certain forms of avant-garde art, Benjamin for an uncritical idea of emancipation through technology, and Brecht for a wooden idea of participatory spectatorship, underlining Adorno's claims that no art form escapes the confines of capitalism. It is this notion that every supposedly emancipatory solution comes with a caveat that attracts Rose to Adorno.

In this context, Jay notes Rose's astute understanding of Adorno and Horkheimer's *The Dialectic of Enlightenment* as drawing on Nietzsche's critique of rationalism to go beyond Marxist discussions of class in analysing fascism. He likewise underlines the differences in Rose's interpretation of Adorno over the years. While in *The Melancholy Science* Adorno's failure to sufficiently engage material politics in his negative dialectics is deeply discussed, he is upheld more positively in *Marxist Modernism*. 'My claim', notes Rose, 'is that Adorno developed a systematic Marxist sociology of art – more systematic and more consistent than anybody else that we've looked at in this lecture series.'

In *The Melancholy Science*, Rose more forcefully underlines the Frankfurt School's fraught relationship with Marxism via Adorno:

> Neo-Marxist, it was not deterred by academic cries against 'materialism' and 'materialist' methods. On the other hand, the School faltered in its attempt to redefine Marxism intellectually and politically for its generation... Instead of politicising academia, it academised politics.

Yet 'the melancholy science is not resigned, quiescent or pessimistic. It reasons that theory, just like the philosophy it was designed to replace, tends to overreach itself, with dubious political consequences.' Such reasoning emphasises the power of critical thought in itself, a philosophical rather than political method enriched by and through dialectical paradoxes. Adorno's morality, according to Rose, 'is a praxis of thought not a recipe for social and political action.'

Most of the debates regarding the relationship between Rose's early and late work (excluding the explicitly theological reading offered by Rowan Williams) hinge on the issue of Rose's Marxism. This includes Osborne as well as Tony Gorman and Martin Jay, for whom Adorno is likewise central.

Tony Gorman holds to the argument that Rose broke with both Adorno and critical Marxism in *Hegel Contra Sociology*. In 'Gillian Rose and the Project of a Critical Marxism', published in *Radical Philosophy* 105 in 2001, he argues that Lukács' three-part 'Reification and The Proletariat' is the centrepiece of Rose's project. Following this interpretation, *The Melancholy Science* is seen to correspond to 'the phenomena of reification' and *Hegel Contra Sociology* to 'the antinomies of bourgeois thought', but Rose never formulated a response to the third part of the essay, 'the standpoint of the proletariat'. Gorman views this as 'the stumbling block of Rose's thought': her lack of an economic analysis and attendant immanent political and philosophical critique echoes her reaction to a similar lack in Adorno's work. On the one hand, Rose embraces Adorno's approach; on the other, she rejects the basically negative stance it suggests. This mirrors the ambivalence towards the political of her own thought.

In this sense, it is interesting how much Rose's broken middle echoes Adorno's negative dialectics. In a 1936 letter to Benjamin, Adorno provides feedback on an early draft of 'The Work of Art in the Age of Mechanical Reproducibility'. In his critique of Benjamin's notion of emancipation in new forms of mass-produced art, Adorno stresses that popular, mass consumed art and avant-garde, autonomous art should be seen as dialectically intertwined: 'Both bear the stigmata of capitalism, both contain elements of change ... Both are torn halves of an integral freedom, to which however they do not add up.' Rose quotes Adorno's 'torn halves' phrase five times in *Marxist Modernism* to explain Adorno's aesthetics, telling her students 'I've probably said it ten times, I can't remember.'

For Adorno, this statement operated on several levels. It describes the rift between the individual and the collective under capitalism, in which societal pressures to see oneself as a unique individual push up against everyone's reduction to labourers and consumers, resulting in alienation. Adorno underlines that this state of affairs leads to a perpetual negotiation of individuals and society that draws on Hegel's dialectic but refuses synthesis. Ethical life, Adorno concludes, is impossible under capitalism. This thought undergirds his idea of negative dialectics, or the idea that truth can only be approached through such negation, contradiction, and non-identity, and sounds quite a lot like Rose's broken middle.

Almost twenty years later, Rose cites his phrase yet again to critique Franz Rosenzweig's engagement in theosophy privileging transcendent justice over immanent politics, arguing, 'Judaism and Christianity emerge as "torn halves of an integral freedom, to which however they do not add up" ... the freedom whose integrity is rent ultimately belongs to God.' In this formulation, she parallels religious traditions under God to ethical life under capitalism to suggest that no religious-theological tradition is absolute. This suggests theology forms part of the aporia between theory and practice.

It also fits with what *Marxist Modernism*'s editors describe as Adorno and Rose's 'aporetic Marxism', or 'a more open and dialectical view of Marxism'. They contrast the acknowledgement that Adorno's pessimistic direction makes it hard to imagine how his work on Marxist theory can connect to political practice with a passage from Rose's *Mourning Becomes the Law*. This suggests that the issues that haunt Adorno's 'torn halves' continue on in Rose's work, even later in her career, alongside and intertwined with theological themes. The editors underline that Rose's broken middle revels in 'stressing the gap between theory and practice, which strain towards each other'. This proposes that Rose's entire oeuvre should be considered a critical Marxist project.

Both Osborne and Gorman's critiques are convincing, the former arguing that the link between Rose's Hegelian Absolute to theological themes undermines critical Marxist readings of her entire oeuvre, and the latter stressing that a hard break in Rose's early and late work mirrors the ambivalences in how Adorno related to material politics. They are persuasive mainly because, like Adorno, Rose did indeed have ambivalence in her own thought, in her case related to both politics and theology. And Rose did indeed ultimately fail to achieve, in Gorman's words, 'a politics of revolutionary transformation.' Investigating Rose's place in Marxist modernisms, critical Marxisms and their afterlives is not a question of strictly categorising her as a thinker, just as the continuous interest in Adorno partially stems from the resistance his isms, aphorias and melancholy potentials poses towards strict categorisation. This parallels how Rose sees the Frankfurt School thinkers discussed in *Marxist Modernism* as hotly deliberating the potential of modernisms and getting much wrong. Yet she concludes that we nevertheless profit from their debates. Rose's fraught legacy asks who and what is allowed to be included in the debate on her place in Marxist thought, provocatively contributing to an ongoing conversation in constellation.

Rachel Pafe

Adorno or Lukács?

Gillian Rose, *Marxist Modernism: Introductory Lectures on the Frankfurt School and Critical Theory* (London: Verso, 2024) 176pp., £17.99 pb., 978 1 80429 011 8

The publication of Gillian Rose's lectures on the Frankfurt School from 1979 gives us the opportunity to evaluate Rose's work and the legacy of the Frankfurt School. Rose's broadly positive account of the Frankfurt School, especially the work of Theodor Adorno, allows us to revisit an interpretation of the Frankfurt School that has become widespread.

The legacy of Rose has been shaped by her often dense and difficult philosophical work combined with the dramatic events of her life – an early death from cancer aged 48 in 1995, the late conversion to Anglicanism, and the relationships detailed in her memoir *Love's Work* (1995). That later work, re-published recently in the UK by Penguin Classics and in the US by NYRB books, has probably done the most to shape her image and legacy.

In theoretical terms she inhabits a complex and unusual position. While these lectures give the impression of a partisan of the Frankfurt School, her first book, *The Melancholy Science: An Introduction to the Thought of T W Adorno* (1978), offered some criticisms of the work of Adorno. It would be her 1981 book *Hegel Contra Sociology* that proved to be her most important work and which cemented her position as a trenchant Hegelian critic of modern philosophy. Convincingly dismissing Althusser in a few pages, the book lambasted the baleful influence of neo-Kantianism on contemporary sociology and philosophy. This is a work of great complexity, but also importance. Compared to many of the recent Hegel 'revivals', such as that claimed by Slavoj Žižek, Rose's work is a model of rigour and analysis. She places Hegel's speculative mode as central and wields that mode as a powerful critical weapon.

After that Rose published a series of books that critique contemporary thought: *The Dialectic of Nihilism* (1984), *The Broken Middle* (1992), *Judaism and Modernity* (1993), and *Mourning Becomes the Law* (1996). While still intransigently criticising the thinkers associated with post-structuralism, these works showed an increasing engagement with religious thought, notably that of Kierkegaard. Rose's trajectory as a thinker was, of course, violently interrupted by her illness and death, but we can see an increasing turn to religious thought to heal the 'broken middle' of modern philosophy. In a way Rose remains with the division of her early reading that brought her into philosophy: Plato's *The Republic* and Pascal's *Pensées*.

These lectures are, in fact, somewhat anomalous to this trajectory. Given in 1979 at the University of Sussex shortly after the publication of *The Melancholy Science* they lack that book's critical bite and show little sign of the rapid turn to Hegel. In fact, what we have here is a fluent account of the Frankfurt School that tells, what is by now, a familiar story. Rose is keen to emphasise two things: the convergence of Marxism and modernism in the Frankfurt School and the importance of the thought of Adorno for its thinking of reification (the turning of social relations into things or commodities) as operating at all levels of society.

The lectures are presented as discussions of the major figures, from Lukács to Adorno, via Bloch, Benjamin and Brecht. According to the editors they give us a more accessible Rose and certainly the tone is more informal and pedagogic than her other published works. The lectures are heavily focused on the Frankfurt School thinkers as analysts of culture, particularly literature and music. The claim is that both Marxism and modernism converge on the need to produce the new to match (or exceed) the development of capitalist society. They share, according to Rose, a common need for innovation. The fusion of Marxism and modernism sometimes leads Rose into errors, as when she supposes that the thinker Ernst Bloch is a composer, confusing him with Ernest Bloch. Her model is Theodor W. Adorno, who is not only a thinker of Marxism as modernism but also a composer and pianist. Rose goes even further by arguing that Adorno's contributions to Thomas Mann's novel *Doctor Faustus* elevate him almost to the status of co-author.

In the story of Marxism and modernism that follows Georg Lukács is the villain and Adorno the hero. Lukács has an honorable role for his discussion of the crisis of the epic and historical periodisation in his early pre-Marxist *Theory of the Novel* (1914) and for his pioneering discussion of commodity fetishism in *History and Class Consciousness* (1923). After that, however, Lukács has nothing to add, or less than nothing. His invocation of the party as the solution to commodity fetishism is dismissed by Rose without putting anything significant in its place and without considering Lukács's own self-criticism. His later turn to realism and hostility to modernism is seen as hopelessly retrograde and Stalinist. Realism is equated to an accommodation with the powers that be and as an endorsement of a conservative ideology, while modernism is seen as a resistance to the culture industry and a radical alternative.

Rose begins her story of Marxist modernism with Ernst Bloch who, while not a member of the Frankfurt School, set it on its way with his embrace of the modernist aesthetics of expressionism. In fact, Rose claimed he 'escaped' Stalinism, when he lived in accommodation with it in the GDR until 1956. This error is all part of the need to blame the later Lukács for being a Stalinist thinker while exculpating the rest of the Frankfurt School. The importance of Bloch, for Rose, is that he presents a vision of revolution as explosive, challenges a model of history as linear, and celebrates Expressionism as the aesthetic of this explosive disruption. Rose certainly argues that Bloch is too extreme in his position and suggests he and Lukács are opposed in ways which miss the core concerns. She does conclude, however, that whatever his errors in emphasising the irrational and decline, Bloch is right in his argument for the non-linear vision of history. The problem is that there is little justification given for this argument.

Walter Benjamin is treated more critically than he usually is in accounts of the Frankfurt School. His embrace of the potentials of technology and popular culture is not treated as alternative to Adorno's high modernism but as a regression that is *too* hopeful. This faith in the potentials of technology is also used as a critical point against Brecht and his influence on Benjamin. While Brecht is called a 'saint' by Rose, she argues that he too is limited in his understanding of a critical realism. Brecht is treated as philosophically naïve and most useful for his criticisms of Lukács. Once again, Adorno is the more likely saint, as his account of Brecht is, for Rose, the best integration of the possibilities and limitations of Brecht's aesthetics.

What is Adorno's position? The importance of Adorno is his argument that commodity fetishism occupies all the levels of the art work, from its genesis to its consumption. There is no easy way out, although we might wonder if there is any way out? The dominance of commodity fetishism is used by Rose to explain Adorno's notorious hostility to popular culture, especially his essay on jazz, but also Adorno's critical remarks on modernism as well. While this is true the difficulty is that there is an imbalance in the account, in which high modernism offers more scope for resistance to commodity fetishism than does popular culture, which gets short shrift. A few times Adorno does discuss popular culture as a site of resistance, but this often seems to be for residual or archaic elements. Rose complicates the image of Adorno's elitism, but whether we can say she truly rescues him from it remains in question. The asymmetry of Adorno's account, and his tendency to see resistance in what lies at the edges of capitalist culture, leave us with an elitism that is only more refined.

The editor's offer a useful phrase when they suggest that Adorno's position amounts to an '"aporetic" Marxism'. What this means is that Adorno does not resolve the contradictions of capitalist society or see the resolution of those contradictions in socialism as possible. Instead, he traces the aporias, the irresolvable contradictions, as the sites of resistance. In this way, with no grounding in the contradictions of reality, Marxism becomes a matter of faith in the face of despair and defeat. There is no doubt that Adorno recognised the deep sense of defeat in the post-war period, but being unable to escape that he left us with no exit.

Rose's *Hegel Contra Sociology* aimed to resolve the impasses of the Frankfurt School, including Adorno, by a new speculative thinking inspired by Hegel. She now took a more critical line on the inability of the Frankfurt School to transcend the limits of capitalist society. Rose also used Hegel to criticise Marx, arguing that he failed to grasp the centrality of culture as a mediating instance. The continuity with Rose's earlier work lies in the attention to culture, but now Rose argues that Adorno is unable to grasp history and abstraction, which are replaced with a Nietzschean 'morality of method'. Adorno repeats the problem of the Lukács of *History and Class Consciousness* of imposing an abstract solution on the problem of reification. If Lukács imposed the party as solution, Adorno imposes this Nietzschean method as a solution. Instead, Adorno's negative dialectics needs to be replaced by a Hegelian speculative dialectics.

The problem is that Rose limits the speculative dialectic to a cultural and phenomenological form. The speculative dialectic is detached from Hegel's metaphysical rationalism, and specifically detached from an objective logic of Being (detailed in Hegel's *Science of Logic*). It is also a reading that does not go into the dialectic of nature. Leaving the dialectic unable to deal with first and last things will then leave Rose vulnerable to them being dealt with by theology.

To return to *Marxist Modernism*, we can note that the dismissal of Lukács and the choice of Adorno creates a difficulty. This is especially true of the dismissal of the later Lukács, who makes powerful criticisms of his own earlier works, both the existentialism of *The Theory of the Novel* and the revolutionary Romanticism of *History and Class Consciousness*, which chime with Rose's doubts. But all Rose can see in the later Lukács is his compromises with Stalinism, his focus on realism as a misunderstanding of modernism, his lack of attention to style, and an inability to grasp capitalist society. This is most evident in her discussion of Lukács's *The Destruction of Reason* (1952), in which she repeats Adorno's criticisms, including the unfounded claim that Lukács calls Freud a fascist. While there are problematic Stalinist elements in *The Destruction of Reason* there are also powerful criticisms of irrationalism, especially of the work of Nietzsche, that the Frankfurt School often treated less than critically.

While it is easy to dismiss the later Lukács, his preference for Thomas Mann over Franz Kafka is one that most would disagree with, we might pause with his realism. First, we need to understand the turn to realism as an answer to Lukács's earlier existentialism and Romanticism (as well as these traits in the later Frankfurt School). Realism is intended to grasp reality, not just as it is but also as it is contradictory and dynamic. For Lukács, following Marx, capitalism is a development that we need to transcend and we need to do so because capitalism cannot resolve its contradictions on its own terms. The power of realism, as an aesthetic, is that it helps us understand this reality. The second point is we need to grasp why Lukács criticises modernism and not assume modernism is just right, as Rose seems to do. For Lukács modernism reflects capitalist reality, but it only offers a limited image of this reality. Like Adorno, it tends to produce an aporetic image of capitalism as a set of unresolvable contradictions.

The issue of Stalinism is real. Lukács agreed with Stalin's argument for socialism in one country and was complicit in Stalinist terror. In terms of realism, Rose argues that 'Lukács and Stalin developed the concept of socialist realism', which suggests a bizarre working arrangement that did not exist. Certainly, Lukács did think realism and socialist realism was the correct aesthetic path. He also argued, after Stalin's death, that the Stalinist version of socialist realism was a kind of revolutionary Romanticism, not actually a realism. For Lukács the cure for the Stalinist version of realism was not less realism but more. It would only be by seeing the contradictory elements of the Soviet system that we could also transcend those limits as well.

This is not to minimize Lukács's compromises with Stalinism, but we must also recognise his later contestation of Stalinism through a return to Lenin. It is, however, to argue that there is more to realism than Rose is inclined to accept. This is also to challenge the broader cultural narrative of 'Marxist modernism' that has come to be the accepted framing for the Frankfurt School. Now modernism itself has receded into the historical distance and been absorbed into the functioning of what Adorno and Horkheimer called 'the culture industry' perhaps we can deepen some of the criticisms Rose poses through the concept of realism. While Rose dismisses realism as a critical tool for its lack of attention to style, a criticism from within modernism, we could ask if the broader remit of realism might draw our attention to the limits of modernism in a more radical way. This is especially true of the point Lukács makes of modernism as a mirror of capitalist reality that can imagine no way beyond reality except in a mystical escape. The oscillation of modernism and the avant-garde between a technophilia and a mysticism is indicative of its inability to grasp the dynamics of capitalist reality as contradictory and transitory. Instead, realism suggests the objectivity of capitalist forms, their inevitable crisis, as well as the necessity that we mediate that sense of crisis through subjectivity.

In this way Lukács's realism answers the problem of his early existentialism and tendency to see the world as hopeless, by arguing that we need to understand the objective dynamics of capitalism and move beyond the sense of crisis and our own despair. It also moves beyond his Romantic invocation of the party as solution in *History and Class Consciousness*. Certainly, his later realism does not mean the abandonment of the party as the necessary collective mediator of social reality, but this party itself has to be attentive to the dynamics of that reality. In literary terms, this is why Lukács turns to the critical or bourgeois realism of the nineteenth century, especially Balzac, as a model. While Balzac is a reactionary, as Lukács knows, as such he is acutely sensitive to social change and tries to map that social change in his sequence of novels grouped as *The Human Comedy*, which provide a rich collective portrait of French society. In the same way a future socialist realism will be more confident in the rise of socialism as a solution, but it will not present this solution as overcoming reality through an act of will. This was the problem of Stalinist social realism, which Lukács would argue was not realistic enough in its hymning of shock workers or the wisdom of Stalin as the means to overcome impasses in social reality. In fact, Lukács would turn to Solzhenitsyn's *One Day in the Life of Ivan Denisovich*, and his other novels, as realist critiques of Stalinism.

All this suggests that we turn a more critical eye on the work of Gillian Rose and of the Frankfurt School in the contemporary moment. The common recognition that Rose's most important philosophical work is *Hegel Contra Sociology* needs to be reinforced and developed through grasping some of the limits of that work. The scope of the Hegelian project and the revisions and expansions of it by Marx, Engels, and the classical tradition of Marxism need to be used here. Also, we need to develop and refine

Rose's powerful criticisms of neo-Kantian legacies, which tend to create fractured binaries and impose solutions by fiat. This can be extended to the legacies of the Frankfurt School, as Rose did, but also to the prevarications and tensions of Rose's own project.

If we do not overcome these limits and these fractures we will be left with the broken middle of our contemporary moment. This involves the celebration of the mystical and the marginal, as with the figure of Simone Weil, described by Rose as an 'angry angel' in *Judaism and Modernity*. Today Rose herself is slotted into the role of Weil: a tragic figure of the philosopher embracing an act of religious conversion in the face of suffering and death. On the other side to the mystic we have the Stalinist image of an orthodoxy that is insufficiently self-critical and unable to come to terms with its own violence, as we find in Domenico Losurdo's *Stalin*. We live in a version of Koestler's choice between the mystical yogi and the Stalinist commissar. While it is possible to identify Lukács as a disguised figure of the Stalinist commissar we would want to suggest that his realism offers a way to mediate and transcend this impasse. Rose was right to point us to the antinomies which structure our thinking and the false solution of the holy city, the mystical or religious, as solution. Beyond Rome and Jerusalem lies a communism that can achieve a properly worldly resolution of the contradictions of the present.

Harrison Fluss and Benjamin Noys

Screwball tragedy

Aaron Schuster, *How to Research Like a Dog: Kafka's New Science* (Cambridge, MA: MIT Press, 2024). 344pp., £27.00 pb., 978 0 26254 354 5

Life is merely terrible; I feel it as few other do. Often – and in my inmost self perhaps all the time – I doubt whether I am a human being.
Franz Kafka to Felice Bauer, July 7, 1913.
One cannot not live, after all.
Franz Kafka, The Blue Octavo Notebooks

In *How to Research Like a Dog: Kafka's New Science*, Aaron Schuster compels us to return to the nuts and bolts of Kafka's work, asking us to relearn our Kafka 'ABCs'. This formula becomes a running refrain throughout the book that alerts us to the crux of Kafka's structural dialectic. Although Kafka is often viewed as a non- or even anti-systematic thinker, it is the wager of the book that if one reads Kafka from the point of view of his fictional philosopher – the dog in Kafka's *Investigations of a Dog* – one sees delineated a contradictory dialectic differentiated from but proximate to a dialectic of contradiction. If we tarry with this contradictory dialectic, we discover Kafka's new science whose ambition is not to become the Queen but 'the demon of the sciences'. The adumbration of this science promises to be a '*folisophie*' (a follysophy) as Lacan has quipped.

Rereading Kafka from the point of his *folisophie* shifts the accent in how we understand the dogmas of Kafkadom. If Kafka's work is usually associated with the 'obscure and unassailable powers' of a 'godless modernity', 'an obscure agency lying beyond this world (the unreachable Sovereign, the inaccessible Law, the absent God, the larger-than-life Father)', Schuster's book demonstrates the problem in Kafka does not lie in a transcendence that confounds but 'the subject's failed insertion into the social world': his characters' inability to assume their symbolic place within the world. The subject *is* this very 'botched entry', which Kafka in a diary entry describes as 'a hesitation before birth.' (In chapter 3, Schuster offers a brilliant interpretation of this diary entry in terms of Plato's Myth of Er and Freud's account of the 'choice of neurosis' [*Neurosenwahl*].) Kafka's characters are not *just* victims of circumstance, determined by inexorable social forces (bureaucracy, the state, the family, capitalism, etc.) beyond their control. Rather Kafka depicts the ways in which his heroes 'self-sabotage', implicating themselves in structures that allow them to encounter the obstacles that drive them, never allowing them to settle into a comfortable place. As Kafka's dog will discover: 'My questions only serve as a goad to myself.' By realising that philosophy '*is the disturbance that it seeks to eliminate*' and by 'cultivating and elaborating the disturbance itself', Kafka's dog becomes exemplary of the way that 'all Kafka's characters ... nurture their derangements and enjoy their symptoms.' *Folisophie* as the demon of the sciences does not seek resolution but disturbance.

The contradictory dialectic, driven not by resolution but impasse, is sustained by Kafka's imaginary effort to recast the function of myth (and thus story telling) through a displacement of its form. (Schuster will subsequently argue that Kafka 'fulfilled the program set out in 'The Oldest System Program of German Idealism', inventing a rational mythology for the twentieth century'.) This is particularly clear in Kafka's stories that rewrite classical mythology. Kafka's reversal, fissure, estrangement and derailment of 'the old myths', as Schuster writes, 'creating an unprecedented mythology oddly conflicted about its mythicality', exemplifies Kafka's approach to the story. Kafka's strategy of neuroticising myth – creating stories, fables, parables that unfold through impasse – serves to locate the birth of a comically tragic subject, making Kafka the inventor of a new genre: the 'screwball tragedy'. This subject and the oddity of its freedom is the 'impossible object' of 'Kafka's New Science': odd and impossible since the freedom at issue is unfree. This new science of unfreedom studies the ways in which the subject trips into being over its own nothingness. Its subsistence and even 'success' consists of a persistent failing that cannot but lead to the failure of this new science. Yet this failure is but the failure of the science of failure and thus a strange success. If Schuster's book is understood as an effort to found a new science, then it is a failure. However, by drawing attention to this persistent failing, the book succeeds in constituting its impossible object. In this sense, Schuster's book is a truly elaborate joke at its own expense. By taking Kafka's 'dog' as its object – or strictly speaking, the simile 'like a dog' – Schuster elaborates an elaborate wisecrack that hinges on a dog whose *sophia* lies in having 'a good nose for cracks' (another of the book's repeated refrains).

This is what it means to be 'a champion of the impossible', as Schuster suggests in a wonderful reading of Kafka's fragment from 1920. The story describes the return home of an Olympic champion swimmer who broke the world record. However, while delivering his victory speech in front of an adoring crowd, he confesses with 'the uncanniness of true candor' (to borrow a phrase from Walter Redfern) that he cannot swim. He has done it; he has broken the record, but it remains nevertheless impossible, for he cannot swim. The story is the purest distillation of what Kafka tells his friend Max Brod: 'You want the impossible, while for me the possible is impossible.' In Kafka, doing and having done – the act – does not make possible. Rather its achievement, amplified by success, serves only to magnify the impossible place of any accomplishment. No victory, no success, no achievement can nullify the impossible. There is no way to escape one's former inability: 'the subject is the irrepressible memory of its anterior impossibility.' To paraphrase an entry in Kafka's notebook that opens Schuster's second chapter, 'Kafka Swims': despite being able to swim 'like the others', Kafka is unable to forget his former inability to swim, so this mere capacity is of no help to him; he cannot swim. To research *like a dog* is a matter of sniffing out this logic, or better, its illogic; Kafka's illness being the leitmotif of the book. According to Schuster, he is the most sublime of obsessional neurotics.

As one can already fathom, Schuster's book is extremely ambitious and very fun, as serious as it is playful. He asks us to read Kafka with an to eye to how Kafka swims. Whether one knows one's Kafka or has just dabbled around the edges, this book compels us to unknow Kafka, asking us to read Kafka while remaining attached to not having read Kafka, and thus requiring that we repeat our Kafka ABCs. Like the late David Lynch, Kafka is an artist whose ambition lies in his dogged effort to repeat the world otherwise, installing the reader within a universe that is not just ordinary but utterly ordinary and not just odd but inveterately so: utterly ordinary and persistently, insistently odd. Dogged in its oddity. Kafka writes the normal with such insistence and persistence, so doggedly, that it loses its normality, shedding in turn its veneer of sanity: the sense of things is loosened if not vacated. As we learn in a chapter dealing with the pleasure of copying, addressing Kafka's relation to Flaubert's *Bouvard and Pécuchet*, Kafka likens writing in a diary entry from 1920 to the act of hammering on a table:

> the wish to hammer a table with painfully methodical, technical competence and simultaneously not to do it,

and not in such a way that people could say, 'Hammering a table is nothing to him' but rather 'Hammering a table is true hammering and at the same time nothing to him', whereby the hammering would surely have become still older, still more real, and if you will, still more insane.

Hammering a table is supposedly a sane thing to do, at least for a judge to bring order to the court, but it quickly loses this veneer if the act exceeds a threshold, if it is done too vigorously, too persistently, if it goes on too long, if it is done too death. Kafka writes, 'Beyond a certain point there is no return. This point has to be reached.' Hammering becomes true hammering and thus 'nothing to him' when it is done with and without a point. The act of hammering becomes all the more pure, but all the more insane. One persists without having a reason to. Persisting without reason is the core conundrum of the Kafkian subject, quintessentially distilled in *Investigations of a Dog*.

Schuster's book is not only itself an investigation of how Kafka writes with a hammer, he himself becomes a little *like a dog*, doggedly hammering away at *Investigations of a Dog* until the point is lost. This is not a criticism. For the point of the book, the persistence in which Schuster hammers away at his concern, is not simply to provide an interpretation of Kafka's story. He does so brilliantly and exhaustively, chasing after the enigma of the tale as a dog chases after its own tail. Rather the pursuit of this story is itself a strategy or device that allows Schuster to pursue the tale by not reaching the point. Like a dog, he does not reach the tip of its tail. As he tells us in the penultimate chapter:

> The dog is not so much the subject matter of this book as its formal axiom, its rule of the game—the means for constructing a labyrinth from which I've tried to find a way out … The dog serves as the absent center that brings together a certain constellation of philosophy, psychoanalysis, art, and literature.'

In terms of Oulipo's literary practice, which Schuster avows, the dog is Oulipian, which is to say, like a rat 'who must build the labyrinth from which [it] propose[s] to escape.' By amplifying one's unfreedom, one frees one relation to the 'un' of one's freedom, becoming a champion of the impossible. For Schuster, the failure of his Investigations to arrive at or reach a point is to the point, since this is what it means to go back to basics, to one's Kafka ABCs, to grapple with what Schuster with Lacan calls the thing-like quality of Kafka's writing, the manner in which it courts and thwarts interpretation, 'stifling the search for meaning it incites.'

The writer Joshua Cohen likens the difficulty of writing about Kafka to 'being asked to describe the Great Wall of China by someone who's standing next to it. The only honest thing to do is point'. This honest act is itself a metonymic procedure. In pointing to the wall, one points to a point, to the bricks and mortar, not to the wall as such (the thing itself, *die Sache selbst*) but to a part that stands in for it. Faced with the wall of Kafka's corpus (not to mention the heap of interpretive detritus amassed at its base), Schuster begins by pointing to one of its most enigmatic partial objects – the story *Investigations of a Dog* – and then doggedly pursues what this act of pointing initiates with this metonymic displacement, pursuing it as an analysand freely associates, as a dog chases after its tail. Constantly returning to this tale, Schuster allows himself to get distracted along the way, to be driven off course. This metonymic procedure is a form of entrapment that nonetheless frees the drives to deviate and drift. Given that the book's 'theoretical' concern is the 'drive' (which Lacan proposed on occasion to translate as *dérive*) – the drive to think, to philosophise, to write – the book approaches its 'object' (which happens to be the impossible object of dog science) in the only way that is faithful to its true character: i.e., through deviation and digression. Only by following these *Umwege* can we catch its drift. The paradox of this methodological procedure consists in pointing to a point, which turns out to be no point at all. More akin to Leibniz's monad, this point includes within its closure, within its constraint, a potential infinity of forking paths. And this makes for a very generous book. There are as many passages through it as pages.

Yet, Kafka's cosmos is not that of Leibniz whose faith in a benevolent master had not been shaken. Leibniz inhabits a world in which the principle of sufficient reason reigns supreme. Faith in reason entails a perfect metaphysical architecture in which the infinity of deviations ultimately converge towards a foundational *Klarheit* that renders the parts compossible with a whole, grasped by a mastermind whose benevolent intentions cannot be ill. Kafka's divine comedy is, as Schuster puts it, 'more vicious.' To borrow a lovely formula that Schuster utilises from the Belgian Germanist Herman Uyttersprot, Kafka's universe is one of *Verwirrung innerhalb der Klarheit* (confusion within clarity)'.

If 'the gods died from laughter' as Nietzsche suggests, when they heard 'an old grim-beard' declare himself to be the one and only God', Schuster writes, 'What could be funnier, and more lethal, than for the gods to find themselves transformed into office managers, and the heavens turned into a gray realm of bureaucratic administration?' Kafka does not announce, however, the death of God but his demotion to the ranks of upper, or even worse, middle management. In the age of management, of capital's infinite bureaucratisation, '[a]uthority becomes murky and diffuse, decentered and ungraspable'. The masters of the universe – addled or outfit in comical fatigues – are themselves slaves to an officialdom they only appear to rule over, their office inseparable from the banalities of the 'office comedy.' Schuster writes,

> The universalization of servitude ('I too am a slave') takes place at the same time that service is separated from the servant, rather than being assigned or guaranteed by a master. Kafkian servants are servants in search of service, workers looking not just for work but for a status or position – a symbolic place – that eludes them, in a world that works by keeping them out of place.

In such a scenario, the figure of the dog becomes the cipher of a problem: what is a dog, at least in the classical sense of 'old faithful', if not devoted to its master? And what is a dog to do not only if there are no good masters but no masters at all? What is one to do in the age of universal abjection, wretchedness, servitude? In an age in which there are no true or good masters, the classical dog's devotion becomes an object of envy. 'Old faithful' holds onto the place of the good and the true. A good old dog if it was to encounter such a master would be able to recognise him by his scent. Yet, Kafka's dog is no ordinary dog, or least he is utterly ordinary and thus totally odd, for he begins to investigate the absence of mastery as such without assigning it a place, sniffing without knowing what it is sniffing, encountering its drive to sniff, its drive to investigate. The dog's nose is no longer directed toward an absent presence (the missing master) but an all-too-present absence (there are no masters). Such a dog – Kafka's dog – is forced to develop a new nose, a nose for the gaps and the cracks. This dog sniffs out the missing, querying its presence, without know *what* is missing. This dog is driven not by what it is searching for but by the search and the research. It begins to research *like a dog*, doggedly returning to a missing place. Kafka's dog becomes 'like a dog', because he is no longer a dog having become dogged in his search and research.

Schuster reads Kafka's 'Investigations of a Dog' as

itself a setup for a joke whose punchline fails to arrive. The punchline is less deferred than simply absent – an absence that once sniffed out becomes overwhelmingly present. Although 'the punchline is never explicitly stated', Schuster writes, 'as soon as one gets it it's apparent everywhere, in the dog's various encounters, the mysteries he confronts, his entire research program. And the punchline is this: dogs do not see human beings.' This blindness is the 'cause' of the dog's search, making the story an exemplary case of *Verwirrung innerhalb der Klarheit*. This reframing of the narrative brings us to the crux of Kakfa's ABCs.

Kafka lays out the A, B and C of his ABCs in a letter to Milena Jesenská from November 1920. In the letter, he describes three concentric circles from the innermost to the outermost. 'A' stands, according to Schuster, for the central authority or the unreachable sovereign, which is often conceived as radically transcendent and withdrawn: 'an obscure agency lying beyond this world': the 'mysterious castle', the 'inaccessible law', the 'the 'unreachable Emperor'; B is the representative of A that bars C's, i.e., the subject's, relation to A. Schuster sums it up as follows:

> At its core is the master (A), who is withdrawn and inaccessible; his will is relayed to the subject (C) via an intermediary (B) whom C must 'trust' to be A's reliable representative. There is no direct contact between C and A, no means of access to the inner circle of Power. The center exerts its force on the self precisely as something opaque and unreachable.

The joke of *Investigations of the Dog*, according to Schuster, is a joke at Kafka's expense. Poking fun at himself, the joke lies in the way that Kafka profanes what at first appears to be utterly mysterious. In this reframing, the strangeness of the dog's account becomes suddenly familiar: the 'fantastical concert' becomes 'a performance of trained circus dogs' and the miraculous dogs of the sky (*die Lufthunde*) are unmasked as lapdogs snatched off the ground by their 'invisible masters'. Yet the 'invisible hand' of the Master (A) never truly appears; it can only be inferred. The dog's own drive to search and research is juxtaposed to the reader's knowing inference. The dog is thus placed in relation to an absent presence (the human hand) *and* a present absence (the actual inscription of this absence that drives the dog to research). What this impasse allows us to see is a drive that is not orchestrated from above but erupts from within. This is the true 'object' of *How to Research Like a Dog*. For it is the dog's drive that places it in relation to a structural horizon that is incomplete. It is not the desire to know but the drive to re-search that makes the dog not just a dog but a dog that is *like a dog*.

Both dog and not-dog, Kafka's dog is driven to locate the obstacle over which it doggedly trips. Failing to coincide with its likeness, Kafka's dog truly lacks consistency. Literature is that practice which consists through a contradictory dialectic in which an image is formed of an impossible act. Kafka's rewriting of Don Quixote is perhaps his most ingenious distillation of this image of impasse. For Kafka (as cited by Schuster), it is Don Quixote's suicide that concentrates the quixotic: 'The dead Don Quixote wants to kill the dead Don Quixote; in order to kill, however, he needs a place that is alive, and this he searches for with his sword, both ceaselessly and in vain.' In this bit of 'metaphysical slapstick', we glimpse the quintessence of Kafka's screwball tragedy. A being that is dead (and thus not a being) wants to kill itself but cannot because it lacks the life requisite to meet the act. Already dead, there is nothing to kill and thus Quixote fails to suicide. The suicidal act necessarily fails, lacking an object, but persists in and through this very failure, giving birth to a life that cannot die because it was never living. This failure to suicide binds the quixotic subject to life through its absence. 'The quixotic suicide', Schuster writes, 'is a torsion of death that keeps reproducing itself as a surplus of life'. Interlocked through an impossible act and bound to himself through this failure, the dead Don Quixote, as Kafka writes, is 'positively bouncing with life.' The quixotic suicide lives to make life absent.

By '*failing to not-live*' the Kafkian subject doggedly pursues a life that is nowhere else but here but nevertheless absent: here and elsewhere. Such a subject gives a new inflection to the ancient task of *learning how to die*. Neither Kafka nor Schuster are one, to borrow a particularly apt pun from Antony Burgess, to *let sleeping dogmas lie*. Kafka's new science and the book that grapples tooth and jaw with its ABCs returns us to the oddity of the place from which one philosophises.

Alexi Kukuljevic

Critical inheritance

Jörg Später, *Adornos Erben. Eine Geschichte aus der Bundesrepublik* [*Adorno's Heirs: A History of the German Federal Republic*] (Berlin: Suhrkamp, 2024). 60pp., €40 hb., 978 3 51843 177 1

In Frankfurt, the news of Adorno's sudden death in August 1969 struck like a thunderbolt. The author, who only twenty years earlier had returned to Germany from exile as a perfect stranger, had in the meantime become something of an icon. His lectures and seminars attracted hundreds of interested attendees, his presence was highly sought after by the media, and his public interventions – raising a critical voice in the desolate theoretical and political landscape of postwar West Germany's economic miracle – had come to exert a remarkable influence. This was no small achievement for a thinker whose prose made no concessions to a general readership whatsoever and who articulated an attitude deeply hostile to all forms of conformism. Yet the shock of his unexpected death was not solely due to his intellectual stature. Around Adorno and the Institute for Social Research, a unique biotope of critical thinking had crystallised, bringing together several generations of intellectuals and theorists: from disciples and young professors of philosophy and sociology to social researchers, assistants and students. Some of them were not merely driven by cultural-theoretical concerns or academic ambitions, but saw in critical theory an intellectual and political endeavour they felt was their own. For all of them, Adorno's death marked a rupture, leaving a void that seemed impossible to fill. In the months that followed, it became increasingly clear that the circumstances which had made Frankfurt a central hub of philosophical and social thought – and one of the main centres of the German student movement – were extraordinarily fragile. Institutionally, Adorno's passing provided an opportunity to turn the page and bring an end to Frankfurt's uniqueness as an enclave of critical theory. Politically, the extra-parliamentary left began to distance itself from Adorno, who was increasingly dismissed as an old-fashioned figure – too rigid and detached from political praxis. As a result, those who sought to continue the theoretical and political positions inspired by Adorno's work suddenly found themselves in a state of uncertainty and apparent marginality. How could they move forward? Was it possible to remain faithful to the master's legacy, or was it necessary to reformulate critical theory to keep it alive? And, if so, on what terms?

Jörg Später, who in 2016 published an excellent biography of Siegfried Kracauer, now offers a comprehensive exploration of the intellectual and theoretical landscape that developed around Adorno in Frankfurt. His book maps Adorno's influence from his return to West Germany in 1949 until the early 1990s, navigating the pivotal moment of Adorno's death and the subsequent dispersion of his disciples. These followers pursued their respective paths across diverse intellectual spheres and theoretical orientations. *Adornos Erben. Eine Geschichte aus der Bundesrepublik* [*Adorno's Heirs: A History of the German Federal Republic*] is, in this regard, a truly monumental work and an indispensable contribution to understanding the trajectories of German critical theory after Adorno. Based on meticulous and well-documented research, Später's work provides a rich and nuanced overview of the broad spectrum of positions that emerged from the Frankfurt milieu. His analysis brings together a wide array of figures with little in common beyond their connection to Adorno. These range from loyal disciples such as Hermann Schweppenhäuser and Rolf Tiedemann to Alexander Kluge, writer and leading figure of the New German Cinema, and the prominent philosopher Jürgen Habermas. It also includes philosophers such as Alfred Schmidt and Karl-Heinz Haag, and figures like Ludwig von Friedeburg, who later became Hesse's Minister of Culture. The book further discusses sociologists such as Gerhard Brandt and Helge Pross, as well as key leftist thinker Oskar Negt, feminist scholar Regina Becker-Schmidt, and the recently deceased Elisabeth Lenk, an unclassifiable disciple of both Adorno and Breton. The complexity of this intellectual landscape is further enriched by Später's inclusion of other critical theory exponents such as Peter Szondi, Hans-Jürgen Krahl, Peter Bulthaup, Günther Mensching, Albrecht Wellmer, Christoph Türcke, Detlev Claussen, and Gertrud Koch, among others. However, one might have expected a deeper engagement with figures from the musical and artistic domains, where Adorno's influence was particularly significant. Similarly, authors such as Ulrich Sonnemann or the pioneers of the New Reading of Marx, Hans-Georg Backhaus and Helmut Reichelt, are perhaps covered too briefly. Despite these gaps, the book's primary focus is on the development of a 'school' around Adorno. Später offers a comprehensive perspective on the diverse and often conflicting positions that claim Adorno's legacy. He convincingly illustrates that this legacy has never been without contention, giving rise to differing interpretations regarding the relevance and meaning of Adorno's thought and critical theory. To fully appreciate the book's achievements and potential limitations, it is essential to recognise that it is primarily a work of intellectual history rather than a theoretical analysis. Drawing from an extensive corpus of texts, unpublished correspondences, and interviews, Später meticulously traces the intellectual and theoretical trajectories of those who once belonged to Adorno's circle. In doing so, he offers a compelling portrait of the evolving landscape of West German intellectual life between 1960 and 1990.

Although it is nominally focused on thirteen 'heirs', this work is not solely centred on individual trajectories. Rather, it reconstructs the contexts of theoretical and intellectual production that enabled these trajectories and shaped their distinct characteristics. A key aspect of this involves highlighting Adorno's own context of intellectual production in Frankfurt. His relationships with his future heirs emerged from various fields of activity. Foremost among these was his teaching, which attracted several generations of students. Additionally, his role as director of the Institute for Social Research introduced new research methods imported from the United States, and this led to the training of young sociologists to apply them. His intellectual and theoretical pursuits, public interventions, and theoretical-political positions within a Cold War-era West Germany – marked by the silencing of the National Socialist past and the economic miracle – also played a significant role. It was these different areas of engagement, rather than a clearly defined set of doctrines and positions derived from his thought, that shaped the character of the 'school' that came to crystallise around Adorno in Frankfurt. Consequently, Adorno's influence did not result in a unified theoretical stance but instead produced heterogeneity. For instance, Adorno's connection with figures such as Brandt, Friedeburg and Pross can only be understood within the context of the Institute's empirical social research work, while his influence on Schmidt and Schweppenhäuser stemmed more directly from his teaching. Meanwhile, individuals such as Negt and Lenk approached him primarily out of theoretical-political concerns, as did Becker-Schmidt later on. Others, such as Habermas, arrived in Frankfurt after completing their doctorates to begin their academic careers as assistants. Adorno's relationship with Tiedemann arose from their shared interest in Walter Benjamin's work, whereas his friendship with Kluge was rooted in personal affinities. In summary, the links between Adorno and his 'heirs' were based on diverse circumstances and interests, not all of which were strictly theoretical in nature. This diversity resulted in highly varied trajectories. Therefore, if one is willing to follow Später in considering this a 'school', the term should always be placed within quotation marks.

Später's book primarily focuses on the fate of this intellectual environment after Adorno's death. The narrative unfolds with the struggle for Adorno's succession at the University of Frankfurt and the Institute for Social Research. Student associations, eager to ensure the continuation of critical theory, demanded that one of Adorno's disciples – Negt, Schmidt, Schweppenhäuser or Haag – take over his chair. However, various factions sought to dismantle what had crystallised around Adorno in Frankfurt. In this context, Habermas's nomination of philosopher Leszek Kołakowski sparked conflict and acrimony among those advocating for Adorno's intellectual legacy, ultimately leading to the students blocking the appointment. Eventually, Horst Baier, a disciple of Helmut Schelsky, secured the position, marking a significant rupture. Additionally, the shift in the Institute for Social Research's focus toward empirical sociology, particularly labour relations and social conflicts – what Später terms a 'proletarian turn in the scientific field' – made it clear that the so-called 'Frankfurt School' had become a thing of the past. Its members were compelled to seek opportunities elsewhere. Indeed, of Adorno's direct 'heirs', only Alfred Schmidt remained at the University of Frankfurt. The presence of critical theory persisted mainly through the seminars conducted by Peter Bulthaup and Günther Mensching, which continued independently even after their temporary contracts ended

in 1976. Critical theorists such as Rolf Tiedemann, Christoph Türcke and Karl-Heinz Haag – who had already left academia – were frequent attendees at these seminars. Hermann Schweppenhäuser, Adorno's devoted disciple, emerged as the central figure in these gatherings. Having secured a position in Lüneburg during the 1960s, he gradually established a working group there. Meanwhile, Habermas had relocated to Starnberg, where he formed a new branch of the Max Planck Institute dedicated to social sciences and began working on what would later become his *Theory of Communicative Action*. Oskar Negt, whose legendary seminars in Frankfurt had attracted hundreds of students in the late 1960s and who had become a leading figure of the new left, eventually accepted a position in Hannover. There, he sought to reunite many of the rebellious Frankfurt students, who had scattered following the untimely death of Hans-Jürgen Krahl, and to lay the groundwork for a new phase of critical theory outside Frankfurt.

The 1970s were dark and hostile years for critical theory, due both to the protest movement's shift towards armed struggle and increasingly anti-intellectualist positions, and, above all, to the official reaction of the Federal Republic, which fostered a climate of persecution against left-wing intellectuals. In this context, Später traces the individual and collective trajectories of Adorno's heirs from von Friedeburg's attempts as Minister of Education in Hesse to implement an educational reform based on participatory and democratic principles – which faced strong resistance and ultimately ended in bitter failure – to the conflicts surrounding editions of Benjamin's works, which continued the disputes that had plagued Adorno in the 1960s, now directed against Tiedemann. Später also examines the consolidation of production contexts for Adorno's heirs in Hannover, Lüneburg and Starnberg, which are portrayed as more 'provincial' environments than Frankfurt. He provides a succinct account of the formation of a 'Frankfurt group' around Schweppenhäuser in Lüneburg, where the latter was able to develop his 'pedagogical eros' and bring together figures aligned with critical theory. Further, the book explores the challenges faced by the Hannover group led by Oskar Negt. Although Negt did not succeed in creating a cohesive school there, Hannover nevertheless provided a favourable environment for collaboration. Peter Brückner worked closely with Negt, along with other figures who had studied in Frankfurt. Among them were Peter Bulthaup and two central figures in exploring the intersection of critical theory and feminism: Regina Becker-Schmidt, who during this period began developing her theory of double socialisation, and Elisabeth Lenk, who, following her work on the relationship between aesthetics, critical theory, surrealism and literature, eventually gravitated towards the feminist magazine *Die schwarze Botin [The Black Messanger]*. Beyond his work in Hannover, Negt played a pivotal role in the Sozialistische Büro group, which, through the journal *links*, became an important reference point for the German left in the 1970s. This group sought to articulate an anti-authoritarian alternative to the increasingly dogmatic and action-driven tendencies of the extra-parliamentary opposition. Negt sent Detlev Claussen, one of his most distinguished doctoral students and a former member of Krahl's group, to contribute to this effort. During these years, Negt also began his collaboration with Kluge, a relationship to which Später devotes considerable attention. This partnership produced key contributions to post-Adornian critical theory, including *Public Sphere and Experience* (1972) and the monumental *History and Obstinacy* (1981).

At Starnberg, Habermas began developing a line of work based on new theoretical coordinates that distanced themselves from Adorno's approaches. In its initial phase, this work was marked by his debate with Luhmann's systems theory. Später highlights the theoretical trajectory of Habermas, noting his growing interest in discourse theory and the study of language theory, while also emphasising his involvement in the theoretical and political disputes within a West Germany that was increasingly shifting to the right. As Habermas's works and public influence grew, a particular reading of the evolution of critical theory began to crystallise around him. In this context, the contributions of Helmut Dubiel and Alfons Söllner stand out. The latter played a crucial role in reviving the legacies of Franz Neumann and Otto Kirchheimer, contrasting their work with that of Adorno and Horkheimer. Meanwhile, Dubiel's *Wissenschaftsorganisation und politische Erfahrung* (1978), translated into English in 1984 as *Theory and Politics. Studies in the Development of Critical Theory*, argued that *Dialectic of Enlightenment* represented a departure from the original critical theory project, a perspective that would exert a decisive influence on the prevailing understanding of 'classical' critical theory both within and beyond Germany for decades. Subsequently, Wolfgang Bonss and, of course, Axel Honneth joined this discourse. Honneth, in particular, examined the evolution of Habermas's work and its divergence from Adorno's ideas in an essay significantly titled 'Von Adorno zu Habermas. Zum Gestaltwandel kritischer Theorie' ['From Adorno to Habermas: On the Transformation of Critical Theory'].

Although, in presenting some aspects of this evolution, Später tends to downplay the role of career strategies and personal interests, his depiction of the disputes that erupted in the 1980s over the meaning and validity of critical theory remains highly compelling. Habermas's project in Starnberg did not reach a satisfactory conclusion, leading to his return to Frankfurt in 1983. He brought with him his monumental *Theory of Communicative Action*, published just two years earlier, which had already achieved global recognition. Of course, for Habermas, returning to the former centre of critical theory after more than a decade could not mean a return to the past. His approach represented a fundamentally different proposal, grounded in new premises. At the same time, he framed it as a 'paradigm shift', suggesting an 'overcoming' of the 'old' critical theory and its aporias. Meanwhile, at a time when French philosophy was gaining increasing international influence, Habermas began to associate Adorno's thought with the same anti-rationalist and politically problematic tendencies he identified in poststructuralism. This inevitably led to tensions. These tensions were particularly evident when, shortly after his return to Frankfurt, he organised the first major conference on Adorno – where, apart from the inaugural lecture by the aging Leo Löwenthal, Alfred Schmidt was the only direct disciple of Adorno to be invited. The *Frankfurter Adorno-Konferenz* in 1983 presented a chorus of voices dismissing the old master as irrelevant and obsolete, while rallying around the theory of communicative action. This created unease, not only among figures like Schweppenhäuser – who had not even been invited – but also among a younger generation of scholars, such as Mensching and Türcke, who continued to see Adorno's critical theory as a viable foundation for articulating a critique of contemporary society. In response to the perceived bias of the Frankfurt congress, the *Hamburger Adorno Symposion* was held in May 1984. In an effort to consolidate the 'invention of tradition' of critical theory in a Habermasian framework, the subsequent years saw a series of major conferences in Frankfurt, including ones on Horkheimer (1985), 'The Frankfurt School and its Consequences' (1986), and *Dialectic of Enlightenment* (1987). This attempt to establish hegemony over the interpretation of the classics and the contemporary relevance of critical theory, in turn, provoked responses such as Detlev Claussen's inaugural lecture in Hannover in 1985 and the 1989 publication of the significantly titled *Uncritical Theory. Against Habermas*. Später interprets these struggles among various heirs and followers as a 'struggle for recognition', playfully alluding to Honneth's famous concept. However, given the asymmetry of power relations – between those imposing their hegemonic, self-serving interpretation of the critical tradition with the institutional backing of the University of Frankfurt and a publishing house like Suhrkamp, and an increasingly prominent figure with significant influence beyond Germany – the title *Critique of Power* might have been a more fitting description.

Without any doubt, the comprehensive, choral perspective presented in Später's book is an invaluable resource for anyone seeking to explore the trajectories of post-Adornian critical theory in the Federal Republic of Germany. The book also addresses the so-called *Historikerstreit* – the heated debate over Germany's National Socialist past – highlighting the crucial role of Habermas's intervention in countering attempts to justify Nazi crimes as a mere reaction to the excesses of communism. However, Später does not confine himself to recounting the well-known aspects of this controversy. His work also sheds light on the significance of discussions about the meaning of Auschwitz, which, since the late 1970s, had been advanced by authors such as Micha Brumlik, Detlev Claussen and Dan Diner, alongside the so-called Frankfurt Jewish group. These circles, building on the contributions of Adorno and Horkheimer, initiated an important process of reflection within the German left on the nature of anti-Semitism, thereby reclaiming another crucial dimension of the critical theory legacy.

Yet, despite its undeniable merits, certain aspects of Später's work are debatable – not only in terms of the figures he prioritises or those he omits, but also in his apparent attempt to downplay Adorno's Marxist roots and their influence on critical theory. In addition, although the book's tone is generally balanced and impartial, the author's inclinations inevitably come through. In this regard, the respect and sympathy with which he treats most of his subjects – including figures as ideologically divergent as Jürgen Habermas and Elisabeth Lenk – contrast with the more critical tone he occasionally adopts when discussing authors such as Rolf Tiedemann or Hermann Schweppenhäuser. Some of Später's reservations about their theoretical and personal choices – such as their willingness to remain in the shadow of their former masters – may be understandable. However, it is telling that the book's harshest judgments are directed precisely at authors whose contributions, while of great significance to the tradition and evolution of critical theory, have received less public recognition.

Probably the greatest contribution of Später's work lies in how its broad perspective transforms and complicates the prevailing understanding of what has come to be called the 'second generation' of critical theory. In the account presented in this book, the widely held belief that a 'Frankfurt School' continued to exist after the passing of its founding members – and that, through successive updates and generational transitions, it has now entered its third or fourth generation – is exposed as a mystification. Später demonstrates how Adorno's death marked a decisive rupture, bringing an end to the intellectual environment that had formed around him in Frankfurt. What emerged from its remnants and the subsequent dispersion of its members was a series of disparate intellectual trajectories, theoretical experiments and controversies with no clear common denominator. In fact, the only unifying element among the figures discussed here is the absent figure of the master – and, in several cases, their relationships with him were shaped more by circumstantial factors than by shared theoretical commitments. In this regard, it is important to emphasise that the history presented in this book is one of Adorno's discipleship within the German Federal Republic, rather than a comprehensive account of the subsequent development of critical theory. This approach intertwines the strictly theoretical dimension with personal, political and institutional trajectories. As a result, the distinctive features of Adorno's critical theory are often blurred. In several passages, Später refers to it as merely a 'style of thinking'. However, such a definition, which excludes any further determination, effectively leads to its dissolution. Even if Adorno's critical theory were reduced to a style of thought, one might still argue that dialectics should be considered one of its defining characteristics – a criterion that would, in turn, exclude a significant number of those presented here as his heirs.

If Adorno's work can be regarded as a living tradition of thought, one capable of leaving an indelible mark on successive generations, then a proper understanding of the subsequent trajectories of critical theory and its potential relevance need not begin with his immediate disciples, nor remain confined to the narrow boundaries of Germany. That would, undoubtedly, be a different story but it is worth remembering that theories may be inherited, but not as possessions handed down through a line of succession.

Jordi Maiso

Waiting for the rupture

Cameron Abadi, *Climate Radicals: Why our Environmental Politics Isn't Working* (New York: Columbia Global Reports, 2024). 192pp., $18.00 pb., 979 8 987 05364 5 pb

In this era of climate catastrophe, there is no shortage of 'what is to be done' style interventions. Like Lenin's famous pamphlet, many focus on laggard class consciousness in a time of looming crisis. The injunction to activists is usually the same: stop what you're doing, comrade, you've misunderstood something.

So it is with Cameron Abadi's *Climate Radicals: Why our Environmental Politics Isn't Working*. The book is a comparison of climate politics in Olaf Scholz's Germany and Joe Biden's United States. Given both eras have just imploded under the weight of their contradictions, the book's timing is slightly unlucky. But more than just analysis, Abadi sets out to address normative questions around climate change and political action. These will undoubtedly retain their urgency in Friedrich Merz's Deutschland and Donald Trump's America.

Abadi is a deputy editor at *Foreign Policy* magazine and the co-host of its *Ones and Tooze* podcast. The latter is structured like a philosophical dialogue – Abadi plays the eager student of economics to Adam Tooze's wise master. Tooze, for those unfamiliar, is a ludicrously prolific professor of History at Columbia University. His name has also become associated with a whole subset of well-educated, youngish men who sought a political home after the failure of the Bernie Sanders campaign. Tooze has described his work as offering a kind of self-flagellating class politics for the professional-managerial class. Given their close working relationship, it is safe enough to assume that Abadi has something similar in mind with *Climate Radicals*.

Abadi argues that democratic politics are creaking under the weight of climate change: as we are seemingly incapable of doing what we all agree is necessary, things are taking on a neurotic tone. *Climate Radicals* is framed as a report on the radicalisation of climate politics in response to democracy's actual and imagined shortcomings. Abadi is quite neat with his definitions. 'Democratic politics' here means electoral politics and the purely institutional management of political antagonisms. He defines 'radicalism' as 'an affinity for solving problems by seeking out their source.' Abadi acknowledges that this could include wildly different kinds of politics: even European Central Bank executives might be radicals according to this definition (albeit technocratic, top-down ones). So he clarifies at the outset that his focus will be on politics that emphasise political purity over compromise, and direct, coercive theories of change.

Abadi devotes much of the German section of *Climate Radicals* to the activist groups Letzte Generation (LG), Ende Gelände (EG), and Fridays for Future (FFF). All three agitate outside democratic politics, which can never give them their desired break with the capitalist system. 'In the process of waiting for that rupture', Abadi empathises, 'they teeter on the brink of hopelessness.' He goes to their training meetings and protest actions, and conducts a series of interviews with various figureheads to better understand their fights and fixations. The portraits he paints do not do the participants any favours.

LG comes off the worst. There is a lot of screaming and supergluing of hands to things. There is very little in the way of ideas or strategy beyond a vague idea about citizen councils elected by lottery. EG seems slightly more coherent, originally aiming to seize control of coal infrastructure from capitalists. But because it remained marginal, it devolved into a sort of think tank of unrealism: one of EG's founders here bewilderingly claims that the German judicial system will legalise the sabotage of fossil fuel infrastructure. FFF, in Abadi's view, is clearly the most legitimate of the three, due to its mass participation in the 2019 climate strikes, its focus on peaceful tactics and its links with the Greens. Abadi, however, casts doubt on FFF's claims to represent the German public, and its emphasis on scientific knowledge at the expense of interests. Through this second error, Abadi claims, FFF shows that it doesn't understand political legitimacy – which in his view stems from the general public feeling that its interests are being met to some degree.

Abadi's portrait of the more respectable Greens is not particularly flattering either. Party leader Robert Habeck is held up as being a more skilful political operator than EG's Tadzio Müller or FFF's Luisa Neubauer but in some ways he is no less ridiculous. Habeck's ponderous enviro-Newspeak – 'the left are the new conservatives', 'only change can preserve what we have' – has become meme fodder for disgruntled environmentalists. Somewhat more scandalously, the Greens gained entry into the now-collapsed German government coalition by not only jettisoning the fossil fuel reduction policies that won them 15% of the vote in 2021, but accepting the *expansion* of domestic gas production. Abadi concedes that 'if you believe politics is fundamentally defined by practical results, Habeck can seem a dangerous distraction, satisfied with self-referential intellectualism rather than outward directed action.'

Abadi does not beat around the bush when it comes

to locating these groups in the social hierarchy: they are people with lots of free time, often led by the children of the bourgeoisie and petit-bourgeoisie. He is particularly scathing about their answer to the redistributive questions of climate politics, such as who will bear the cost of the green transition. FFF's Luisa Neubauer relegates this task to faraway, credentialled scientific professionals – a prospect Abadi thinks will (rightfully) not sit well with ordinary people. Abadi also rejects Habeck's first person plural pronoun answer to the question, arguing that

> The term "we" obscures as much as it reveals. It's Habeck and the government he's serving that will decide exactly who will be poorer. This is where the intellectual exercise of dialectic meets the hard constraints of material politics. Who should pay, and how much, for the investments necessary to transition to renewable energy?

But the biggest criticism Abadi lobs at all the German groups he profiles – whether inside, outside, or straddling democratic and radical politics – is that for all their efforts, they have achieved nothing concrete at all.

Counterposed to this gloomy assessment of German climate politics is Abadi's somewhat surprised take on the situation in the United States. The US faces the same international problem that all industrialised nations do: why make the expensive first move on the green transition and have your competitors reap the benefits? The US also fosters more severe domestic democratic obstacles to any green transition: incentivised competition between stakeholders, and red tape that allows fossil fuel companies to litigate green projects to death before they begin.

Into this toxic brew shuffled Joe Biden's Inflation Reduction Act (IRA), which jointly promotes carbon-neutral and carbon-intensive energy production, wagering that the market will ultimately phase out the latter. Somehow, this very 'democratic' approach won the support of climate radicals like the Sunrise Movement – a rough US equivalent of Germany's FFF. It succeeded, Abadi claims, largely because it is all carrot and no stick. This is not to say, he admits, that the IRA is problem-free. On the contrary, the unlikely coalition supporting it began straining almost immediately, and even its Republican beneficiaries immediately declared their intent to kill it if possible (a prospect now imminently plausible). Perhaps most troubling, Abadi suggests, is the centring of the US-China conflict in the IRA. Indeed, of what value are massive concessions to the fossil fuel industry, if they must be accompanied by beating the drums of global war?

In light of the relative failures of the German and US efforts to curb climate change, what does Abadi think is to be done? *Climate Radicals* suggests that we must accept the limits of our capacity to transform the world and embrace a cognitive dissonance he terms 'negative capacity.' The emphasis in terms of public policy should now move to a non-normalising adaptation that both accepts the failure of and continues the climate struggle; both aims to prevent and learns to live/die with global warming.

This normative conclusion is unsatisfactory. First, isn't experiencing cognitive dissonance what most people are already doing in response to the climate crisis? Abadi himself concedes that it is a small minority engaging in manic, ostentatious displays of climate radicalism, and that ordinary people are clearly already reconciling the climate crisis and their own perceived interests in various ways. Second, 'adaptation' no less than 'prevention' demands a question be answered that Abadi accused Neubauer and Habeck of trying to paper over: who will pay for it?

Thirdly, if it set out to find 'why our environmental politics isn't working', *Climate Radicals* instead answers Matthew T. Huber's question in *Climate Change as Class War* (2022). Huber asked 'what agent of change could actually deliver the transformations we agree are necessary to address climate change?' If Huber provides an answer in the positive, Abadi provides one in the negative: certainly not the professional-managerial class! In a recent episode of Abadi's podcast, Adam Tooze suggested that the working class materially experiences professional-managerial class domination as more directly oppressive than capitalist exploitation. Whatever the truth of this, it echoes Catherine Liu's argument from *Virtue Hoarders: the Case Against the Professional Managerial Class* (2021). Like Liu, Tooze argues that working class hatred of the PMC has solidified into reactionary anti-authoritarianism, which pro-fossil fuel figures like Trump can exploit. In terms of its proclivity for histrionics, Liu posits that

> the PMC reworks political struggles for policy change and redistribution into individual passion plays ... if its politics amount to little more than virtue signalling, it loves nothing more than moral panics to incite its members to ever more pointless forms of pseudo-politics and hypervigilance.

Abadi's *Climate Radicals* certainly fits with Liu's grim assessment, with its focus on the cringeworthy and fruitless antics of a layer of bored-but-stressed elites.

Finally, and connected with the previous point, Abadi's method poses something of a false dilemma. Is our choice really between the children of the German bourgeoisie with their pitiable theatrics or American capitalists demanding all carrots and no sticks? Consider for a moment the campaigns to stop the flow of capital into the Keystone XL pipeline or Australia's East-West Link toll road project. In 2014-15 both movements mobilised thousands of ordinary people in direct confrontation with big polluters; roped in blue collar transit unions to their cause by dovetailing 'bread and butter' issues like well-paid jobs for members with social demands like a tolerable living environment; forced ruling political parties into calculated backdowns; and re-routed tens of billions of investment dollars to socially necessary projects. Are victories like these permanent? Not at all – they're immensely fragile. But if we acknowledge their existence, a tougher agent of change rears its head. And when it does, Abadi's political quietism starts to look increasingly lacklustre.

Chris Dite

Proletarian tectonics

Maria Chehonadskih, *Alexander Bogdanov and the Politics of Knowledge after the October Revolution* (Switzerland: Springer Nature, 2023). 289pp., £94.99 hb., 978 3 03140 238 8

Revolutions, like earthquakes or volcanoes, can act like dramatic forces that reshape life on a planetary scale. A year after the 1917 October Revolution, Bolshevik philosopher Alexander Bogdanov attended the first conference of *Proletkult* (Proletarian Cultural-Enlightenment Organisations), distributing reproductions of the prehistoric wall paintings in the Altamira Cave — images of steppe bisons, boars and human hands. He insisted that understanding the life experiences of Palaeolithic hunters connected Soviet workers to the past: 'Comrades, we have to understand: we do not only live in a collective of the present, we live in cooperation between generations'. In his writings, Bogdanov marvelled at mediaeval weaponry displayed in a museum: 'On seeing the coats of armor, shields, simple and two-handed swords, a modern man cannot help but be amazed at the long-gone heroic race'. Would a worker in a Leningrad factory be able to wear such a harness? For Bogdanov, communism is not only a task of the present but a collective labour of life uniting comrades across time.

In *Alexander Bogdanov and the Politics of Knowledge after the October Revolution*, Maria Chehonadskih brilliantly reveals how the October Revolution marked a tectonic shift reconfiguring political, social, epistemic, aesthetic and ecological plates. Revolutionary politics strove to create a new post-humanist environment – a communist earth. Against the longstanding dismissal of Soviet theory as crude, reductive and totalitarian, Chehonadskih's archeology of knowledge reframes the post-revolutionary era as a laboratory for experimenting with new modes of thinking and living collectively. Only now, perhaps, does the full picture – a kind of Soviet cave painting – begin to emerge from the shadows of the past century. In what has already become a seminal introduction to Soviet philosophy, Chehonadskih's book brings lesser-known theories, such as Bogdanov's *tektology* and *empiriomonism*, into contemporary debates about economic planning, systems theory, nonhuman agency and artificial intelligence. She reinterprets the October Revolution as a shift from a human-centred worldview to an 'exposition of processes from different angles, positions, and sides', emphasising more-than-human ways of seeing and thinking.

Inspired by Bogdanov's fascination with the Altamira Cave, her account suggests that revolution was not merely a break with the past, driven by future-directed teleology, but a *metabolic process* of gradually reorganising material structures and patterns of thought. She uses geological metaphors to describe knowledge as skeletal fossils and 'residual sedimentations of the products of exchange between matter and energy'. By excavating and rewiring these energetic exchanges, she reveals an ecosystem of material interrelations between humans and the environment at the heart of the Soviet project. Her meticulous excavation of early Soviet ecology has great urgency amidst today's climate change and fossil-fuelled capitalism. Bogdanov's vision of socialist planning as an intelligent system of equitable distribution is not just an archeological relic; it remains very much alive in current ecosocialist discourse.

Chehonadskih avoids the typical trope in Soviet historiography of contrasting creative thinkers like Bogdanov against a dull backdrop. Rather than treating Soviet theory 'as a lake out of whose dark and muddy waters a researcher may or may not get a very good fish', her book stirs the waters, plunging into the depth of post-revolutionary thought as it emerged from the recursive interplay of avant-garde culture, environmentalism, politics and scientific experimentation. Instead of focusing on exceptional individuals deviating from totalitarian state discourse, she reconstructs an entire ecosystem of Soviet thought. Her approach aligns with post-revolutionary efforts to transform 'the environment as a whole, not a human as a particular unit within it'. The political focus of Soviet theorists of the 1920s, she argues, was to establish a universal proletarian science operating on all scales, from the microscopic to the planetary.

Her book seeks to 'reactivate the epistemological line in the Soviet tradition' buried beneath layers of history, fragments of which have only 'been excavated in order to support particular statements, trends or ideological propositions'. She argues that the ship of post-revolutionary theory, unknown to its builders, can only be reassembled 'retrospectively because it did not exist as a ready-made construction during the first decades of the Soviet experiment'. In doing so, she gathers a lost canon, including thinkers like Andrei Platonov, Nikifor Vilonov, Varvara Stepanova, Anatoly Lunacharsky and Sergei Tretiakov. Opening with a reexamination of Bogdanov, the book situates his philosophy within an intertwined history of Marxism and empiricism ('Empirio-Marxism') in the aftermath of the October Revolution. The introductory section breaks new ground by challenging the reduction of Soviet theory to dialectical materialism repositions Bogdanov's theory of organisation as an environmental paradigm, and dispels persisting myths linking Bogdanov and Platonov to Russian religious mysticism and cosmism. It lucidly traces how different conceptions of materialism became politically and ideologically explosive after the October Revolution.

Empiricist discourse, especially Bogdanov's empiriomonism, was one creative philosophical project that fell through the cracks of history. Before Lenin's *Materialism and Empirio-Criticism* (1909) became authoritative in the 1920s, Empirio-Marxism, a fusion of Russian Machism and Marxism, dominated Soviet philosophy. Bogdanov's empiriomonism infused Marx's materialism with an empiricist theory of knowledge, gleaning concepts like 'energy' from modern physics to create a philosophical environmentalism that inspired the artistic avant-garde. Chehonadskih examines how Bogdanov's empiricist philosophy became enemy number one of Marxism-Leninism. His socialist science of organisation, *tektology*, is presented as an epistemological framework that spans political economy, the human body, labour and the environment. Chehonadskih distinguishes tektology from dialectical materialism (*Diamat*), arguing that while Diamat dissolves contradictions in a 'magic of dialectics', tektology explores the relational structures of self-organising systems, offering a distinct conception of system:

> Systems not only progress, they also regress and decay. This decay is not seen as a contradiction which is to be overcome and sublated. It can coexist with progress and stagnation. Dialectical materialism is lineal and flat. It has no topology or volume. It treats the environment as a container of inner drives that follow a predictable pattern of transformation. Tektology considers what articulates parts and wholes and how they interact and mutually act on each other.

Orthodox Diamat sees the individual as shaped by its environment, reacting to external stimuli (e.g., Pavlov's reflexology experiments with dogs). In contrast, Bogdanov views individual and environment as a complex network of recursive processes: 'there are no absolute breaks in the web of life'. Chehonadskih argues that Bogdanov should be recognised as an epistemic precursor to cybernetics and ecology. Rejecting linear, teleological progress, Bogdanov focuses on varying intensities and degradations. Tektology offers an organisational systems theory that transcends mind-body dualism, placing life within a monistic framework. Rich with environmental metaphors like 'dynamic equilibrium, biophysical co-operation, mutualism, and even distribution', tektology was fatally 'tested' in Bogdanov's blood transfusion experiments which cost him his life in 1928.

For Chehonadskih, empiriomonism 'reflects what can be seen and from which angle and how these angles coordinate and resonate in the environmental mapping of processes'. This ties into a vision of planetary communism where socialist principles function at the level of ecosystems. Chehonadskih links Bogdanov's ideas to a specifically *Soviet Anthropocene* which aimed at a proletarian ecology. After the Revolution, socialist society 'has been placed in a wider environment where biophysical and geological entities co-evolve and form symbiotic structures with the human world'. Bogdanov's post-humanist empiriomonism stemmed from 'the discovery that every organism resembles a system ... which in itself is an environment for something else' – what Chehonadskih calls an 'ontological environmentalism' entwining matter and mind. In Bogdanov's tektological grid, everything is an active part of a larger network.

In a letter to Bogdanov, Nikifor Vilonov, co-founder of the Capri Party School, argued that a true 'philosophy for the proletariat must connect with the new streams of energy spilled on forests, rivers and fields in the form of woodcutters, carpenters, peasants, etc.'. Chehonadskih highlights Machian environmentalism as a key influence on proletarian ecology, rooted in the factory and railway. Chapter 2, 'Strategic Unity of Marxism and Empiricism', examines Bogdanov's organicist systems theory, where bodies, organisms and the environment mutually shape each other. Empiriomonism transforms nature into a construction site, offering a framework for understanding 'how things organise the human world and how the human world organises things'. Matter is structured into 'series, complexes, and systems', where perspectivism becomes central: 'everything relates, and everything is relative'. Parts of the whole reflect one another, such as 'an affect in consciousness ... or an organ in an organism'. All elements together form the environment as a totality of reflexive processes, 'a chaos of elements in the precise meaning of that word.' It is the medium of 'life forms in motion' organised in series like the 'visual, tactile, and acoustic series', connected by *parallelism*. For instance, the series of labour organises the worker's hands, tools, materials and environment into a processual whole. Certain nodal points densely connect complexes, such as 'the human "I"', a lived experience linked to another 'I', forming points of intensity.

Chehonadskih aligns Bogdanov's process ontology with Lev Vygotsky's psychology, with both challenging Lenin's theory of reflection. For Bogdanov, reflection (*otrazhenie*) is 'the chain of feedbacks and interchanges in the structure of experience and life', shaped by the processes of both reflecting and being reflected – everything reflects. Vygotsky's cultural-historical activity theory suggests that thinking reflects bodily affects through the interactivity between body, mind and environment. Vygotsky's enactive view on thinking is revisited in more detail in a new selection of his works edited by Myra Barrs and John Richmond. A clinician at the Moscow Experimental-Defectological Institute, Vygotsky argued that thinking emerges not from the brain alone but through collective social activity. Criticising Pavlov and Bekhterev's reflexology, which reduced subjectivity to conditioned responses, Vygotsky proposed a system of interactions between subjects and their environment. Grounded in Marx's philosophy of *Tätigkeit*, Vygotsky's theory of mediating activity emphasises the dynamic relationship between humans, tools and their social and natural milieu. In *The Heart of the Matter: Ilyenkov, Vygotsky and the Courage of Thought* (2023), David Bakhurst brilliantly reconstructs how Soviet activity theorists such as Evald Ilyenkov viewed transforming nature as 'a semiotic act: by acting on the world, human beings endow their natural environment with meaning'.

Bakhurst suggests that Soviet ecology can be captured in Vygotsky's concept of activity, which transforms an 'inanimate lump of matter' into 'a tool'. In the tool, matter becomes cultural and social – an extended organ of human thinking. As Bakhurst states, 'we have to look beyond the human head'. Activity, inherently anti-Cartesian, gives meaning to the environment. Thinking is collective interactivity: 'through her life-activity the individual puts her very life into the world.' It not the environment that 'produces' the person, but the collective shaping the world through overlapping mediation processes, 'like a peculiar stamp impressed on the substance of nature by social human life-activity'. While Chehonadskih emphasises material structures, Bakhurst highlights the importance of activity (*deiatel'nost'*) in rethinking Soviet ecologies. Activity as a productive ecological episteme is also central to Alex Levant, Kyoko Murakami and Miriam McSweeney's *Activity Theory: An Introduction* (2024). Read alongside Chehonadskih, the volume highlights the role of activity, or forms-in-motion, in socialist life-building.

While Chehonadskih, drawing on Bogdanov, views infrastructures and skeletal forms as the 'embryo of a new collectivised life', activity theory offers a dynamic ecological framework where cognition and agency are inseparable from collective activity rooted in a shared lifeworld. For Ilyenkov, matter itself is active – matter thinks and thinking matters. This opens new ways of thinking about the environment in non-individualised terms, including through materials and tools. As Bakhurst and Levant et al. convincingly demonstrate, Soviet materialism can enrich posthumanist ecologies by emphasising labour and the material interactivity of human and more-than-human beings. An activity framework might also shift perspectives on Bogdanov, who views the environment as 'a battlefield of collective labour, in which human activity is opposed to the elemental resistance of nature', as Chehonadskih puts it. In his socialist process ontology, nature is not inert matter but self-organising activity.

Chehonadskih masterfully navigates the ambiguity of Bogdanov's proletarian ecology: Empiriomonism envisions a dynamic ecosystem shaped by human activity, yet also ties labour to the exploitation of nature, a theme explored further in his science fiction. In *Red Star* (1908), ecological disaster on Mars and resource exhaustion depict industrialisation extending into space colonisation, driven by coal, oil and a 'grandiose, "systematic" conversion of energy', where natural forces are transformed by 'the forces of the labouring collective'. Machinery, organisms and labour form an energetic metabolism. Chehonadskih reinterprets Bogdanov's notion of *stikhiinost'*, usually translated as 'spontaneity' in Lenin's political theory, as a force ranging from lack of control to nature's negative power. *Stikhiinost'* represents 'a lesser or minimal organisation, the chaos of elements that the environment itself embodies', opposing the creative force of life that enables reorganisation and change.

For Bogdanov, communism is the collective 'development of the plasticity of life' through the organisation of activity via 'labour technic'. His empiriomonism is a proletarian 'ontology of the environment', where living beings adapt to their environment through labour, with all life forms, cells to humans, sensing, reflecting and self-organising. In Bogdanov's energetic metabolism of nature, the human 'I' holds no special status, being simply a higher degree of organisation. His monism views nature as 'an infinite series of complexes ... "being reflected" in one another', with the environment as a medium of self-organising activity. In *The Dialectics of Ecology* (2024), John Bellamy Foster has critiqued the 'flat ontology' of posthumanist ecology, which ascribes agency to 'everything from microbes to clouds'. He argues it leaves no space for political action, reducing the world to 'infinite webs of vital assemblages ... circulating nomadically on the same ontological plane without essential order or meaning'. Indeed, Bogdanov's tektology, a posthumanist ontological environmentalism, 'does not consider it absurd to connect the cobblestone, the dream and the telegraph signal together' (Chehonadskih), but does this imply a flat ontology? If everything exists in series, what organises those series into an ecosystem?

The third chapter, 'The Science of Organisation', explores how Bogdanov's tektology offers 'a cybernetic understanding of the organism-machine relationship, guiding a Marxist explanation of how living and artificial systems converge and arrange themselves into a mode of production'. Refuting Foster's claim, Bogdanov's system science rejects placing all living things on the same ontological plane. Emphasising the relationality of series, it favours process over dialectics. Unlike Engels's *Dialectics of Nature*, which sees a grain of wheat negating itself in a plant, tektology examines relational processes, such as the 'contact of grain with the activities of soil, ... the interaction between living and inorganic activities'. Further, it recognises distinct forms of 'organisedness' – crystals, machines and plants – within an ecosystem. Bogdanov's material collectivism breaks down physiological boundaries, enabling biophysical cooperation between humans, animals and plants to counter the destructive elementality of nature. Chehonadskih cites Soviet biologist Boris Kozo-Polyansky, who reinvented cell theory, emphasising 'the synthesis of organisms into symbiotic systems' as the motor of evolution. Kozo-Polyansky's *Symbiogenesis. A New Principle of Evolution* (1924) gives a vivid image: 'a palm tree peacefully growing by a brook, and a lion, hidden in the bushes ... ready to pounce on an antelope'. What makes the palm tree peaceful and the lion violent? Foreshadowing recent research into symbiosis and mututalism, Kozo-Polyansky explains:

A palm tree is peaceful and passive exactly because it is a symbiotic system; because it contains an entire crowd of tiny green toilers, the chloroplasts. They work and feed it. And a lion feeds itself. But let us imagine that a chloroplast is placed in every one of a lion's cells, and I do not doubt that this lion will then calmly lie next to the palm, and the only other thing it might need would be a little water with mineral salts in it.

As Chehonadskih notes, 'Bogdanov dreams of turning lions into palm trees, ... of placing a chloroplast in every lion's cells'. By becoming a plant, the lion evolves into a peaceful comrade of the antelope. This reflects Bogdanov's view of ecosystems as dynamic equilibriums (*podvizhnoe ravnovesie*), where 'material and energy exchange between complexes and their environment' constantly renews itself like a waterfall. Organisms and their milieu engage in recursive interactions, each acting as both mould and material. Bogdanov's blood transfusion experiments aimed to transfer vitality, immunity and physical traits between organisms, ultimately leading to his death from tuberculosis after a contaminated transfusion. Rather than dismissing Bogdanov's pseudo-scientific blood experiments, Chehonadskih reinterprets them as promoting 'biophysical cooperation' in line with modern co-evolution theories, which focus on reciprocal interactions and mutualism. Bogdanov's ontological environmentalism stemmed from a neglected tradition of dialectical biology: His Lamarckian views on heredity were part of debates on genetics in the 1920s which paved the way for Lysenko's anti-Mendelian doctrine. Bogdanov, however, was far from being a proto-Lysenkoist. Chehonadskih aligns tektology instead with contemporary ideas of symbiosis, highlighting the reciprocal influence between human evolution and the environment.

Chehonadskih defines Bogdanov's biopolitics as 'technics for the communist use of the body'. The chapter 'Proletarian Monism' examines Soviet life-building (*zhiznestroenie*) as evolving from a metaphor of manual labour to 'an epistemic figure' linking 'revolutionary reconstruction, workerism, and biopolitical constructivism'. Life-building, an inherently ecological concept, 'reached down into the deeper skeletal layers of transport, production, distribution and city planning'. She contrasts Bogdanov's 'world-building activity' with Taylorist labour control and critiques Aleksei Gastev's biomechanical system as fanatically deterministic and reductionist. Like tektology, proletarian art organises materials into series, collectively shaping the new communist environment: 'The art of walking and talking, of arranging things and the social environment, becomes a common social practice'. The recreation of life, embodied in the Soviet new person, involves mastering biomaterials like breathing, circulation, digestion and reproduction. As Trotsky noted in *Literature and Revolution*, even 'purely physiologic life will become subject to collective experiments'.

The proletarian body, joined with technology and machines, reshapes both itself and its environment, a view central to Proletkult, the radical culture organisation founded by Bogdanov. Proletkult aimed to create socialist collectives free from exploitation, competition and class struggle, envisioning a 'cooperative comradeship of people' where mutual relations and life organisation were consciously created. Proletarian art, like tektology, sought to promote collectivism through labouring bodies, integrating art into everyday life. In 1918, Proletkult's press organ, *Gorn* (Furnace), declared that 'the proletariat will carry art into the streets', taking art from museums to factories. Theorists like Boris Arvatov criticised bourgeois art as 'soilless', advocating for art rooted in proletarian monism. Chehonadskih shows how this environmentalist vision influenced knowledge production, such as the *Great Soviet Encyclopedia*, which aimed to create a new science from the point of view of the working class.

Soviet life-building was a revolutionary remaking of the environment. Material structures embodied this process, with Sergei Tretiakov calling for art to engage with 'the life of the material itself'. Close to Bogdanov's tektology, socialist art emphasised tectonics, which Aleksei Gan described as 'eruptions emanating from the core of the earth'. Both envisioned communism as a force inscribed into the planet's history. Tectonics, like drifting plates or volcanic eruptions, operates with the 'plasticity of form'. Unlike French structuralism, Gan's notion of structure is material, organic and plastic, echoing Bogdanov's view of organisation as life's organic skeleton. Chehonadskih envisions proletarian culture as a 'socio-environmental network' in which things (*veshch*) become comrades, free from alienated labour. Proletarian literature shifts from the traditional novel to a 'conveyor belt' where 'forests, bread, coal, iron and the factory' become main characters, embodying class relations and collective life. Sergei Tretiakov called for children to write biographies of the objects in their pockets, embracing monism where multiple perspectives are used to dissolve fragmentation. Monist strategies are also employed in works by Eisenstein, Rodchenko and Platonov, with a shared interest in unusual angles, multiple viewpoints and overlapping perspectives. The view of the labouring body is anti-Ptolemaic – the individual worker is not a sun, but a common planet in a communist cosmos.

In the recently translated *Mimesis: The Literature of the Soviet Avant-Garde*, Valery Podoroga shows how Rodchenko's angle-technique creates a 'fleshless eye' that sees beyond human perspective, echoing Vertov's 'kino-eye' concept. Podoroga's notion of the 'techno-environment' blurs human-machine boundaries, presenting humans as part of a socialist world shared with factories and locomotives. His ecology of technology highlights 'our own artificiality as living beings', contributing to current debates on AI. Chehonadskih, drawing on Podoroga, argues that Vertov's mechanical eye moves through the 'molecular movements of time, space and matter', navigating the cracks of socialist construction. This multiplicity of perspective eventually solidified into Stalin's absolute gaze. Closely analysing Rodchenko's photo series on the White Sea-Baltic Canal construction by Gulag prisoners, she unveils how avant-garde life-building gave way to Stalinism. While Podoroga identifies subversive potential in 'negative mimesis' (imitating oppressive language), Chehonadskih states that the communist gaze ultimately abolished itself under Stalinist surveillance.

The sixth chapter, 'The Encyclopedia of Poor Life in Platonov's Proletarian Literature', offers a brilliant reading of Platonov's work through the lens of Bogdanov's tektology and posthumanist ecology. In Platonov's proletarian cosmos, humans, plants, machines, and even a 'working-class bear' and 'class-conscious horse' collaborate. *The Foundation Pit* features a 'bear-blacksmith' who works long shifts and despises kulaks. What matters, Chehonadskih notes, is not whether the bear is human or animal but 'what the bear does in the smithy'. Platonov's barren landscapes are raw material for a more-than-human 'labour of life' where 'poor life' emerges from 'earth, dirt and seeds'. Chehonadskih contrasts Bogdanov's focus on the 'built environment of industrial society' with Platonov's broader, posthumanist vision of planetary socialism. Platonov extends 'comradeship to

animals, plants and the earth', seeing the environment as 'a collective body'. For Platonov, literature must 'bear the trace of life and labour', capturing revolutionary realities as they unfold: 'A hungry peasant, the disappeared proletariat or a death after an unsuccessful blood transfusion are slips in the discourse and traces of concrete life'.

Podoroga, on the other hand, reads Platonov's novels as a battle between nature and machine, with interconnected elements hardwired in a textual machine. In *Chevengur*, the revolutionary machine is a system of working parts: 'Rosa Luxemburg's "grave" – Revolution – Horse (named 'Natural Force') – Rider (cavalryman Kopenkin) – Steppe'. A machine is 'society's material unconscious' where the human form evolves into a machinic being. In this posthumanist take on revolution, the machine not only reworks the human but also blurs the boundary between nature and technology, positioning itself as part of the ecosystem. Platonov's cosmos is a desolate space, filled with 'abandoned villages, dry riverbeds, black wounds of ravines'. His universe teems with revolutionary machines: organic, poor, desiring, reproductive, panoptic, human, locomotive ... In this world, humans are 'machine-beasts', taming technology by turning machines into natural beings. The machinisation of nature creates a 'human-less' new nature. The empty steppe becomes the stage for a 'grandiose machinic reorganisation of nature' through a 'cosmic *Megamachine*, a collective Body for each and for all', ultimately erasing the 'evil of bourgeois individuation'.

This final metabolism marks the disappearance of the human, where dust and new nature prevail. Humanity will 'stop the movement of the planets, change the trajectory of comets, transform the environment, the conditions of labour' and its own nature. As Podoroga asks, 'what is Revolution, if not the process of creating a new reality with a fantastic megamachine?' Platonov's machines recover energy lost in the struggle with nature, with literature acting as an 'electromagnetic resonator' that converts sunlight into energy. He believed 'the greatest energy lies at the heart of matter'. For Platonov, 'machines are our poetry and the work of machines is the beginning of proletarian poetry, which is itself an uprising of humanity against the universe'. Podoroga sees revolution as an optic rupture, a 'catastrophe of perception', with communism as 'a new form of universal organisation of matter'. Platonov's planetary vision, in Podoroga's eyes, is encapsulated in his story 'The Descendants of the Sun' (1920s), where the lone watchman of a deserted earth witnesses the arrival of ancient time as glaciers move south and birch trees grow toward South Asia.

Podoroga suggests that 'Platonov's characters cannot live as individual bodies, but only as part of complex conglomerations, colonies, masses, where a particular body breathes the breath of other bodies and gets energy for life or loses it thanks to a multitude of other bodies'. Chehonadskih sharply criticises his interpretation for dissolving perspectivism into some sort of 'Deleuzian immanent materialism'. Rather than simply observing 'the chronicles of revolutionary events in an objective manner', Platonov 'actually organises a proletarian point of view on the social totality'. For Platonov, she insists, people are never merely a colony or multitude: 'Platonov zooms in to the conglomerates and observes a subject and a singularity in it … in Platonov's novels, oppressed others have found … an idea of philosophical thinking that could only have arisen in the revolutionary period'. The poor make themselves, she claims, against their environment. Platonov's ecology for the proletariat, she argues, can only be fully understood through the lens of Bogdanovian perspectivism:

> The proletarian point of view becomes visible as soon as we consider the embodiment of labour in the exploitation of humans, animals and nature, as soon as we find the traces it leaves on bodies and minds. The proletarian point of view in Platonov coexists with a bourgeois and normative perspective, so much so that the same subject in his text can be considered from different observing points.

She argues that while tektology is subjectless, focusing solely on 'the systems of equilibrium and degrees of organisedness', Bogdanov's politics remain 'subject-oriented'. The proletarian ecology he developed after the Revolution strove for 'a new form of comradely relation' aligning 'with the definition of a social system as a complex unity of things and people'. Rather than dissolving the individual into a faceless collective, Chehonadskih sees Platonov, too, as a philosopher of proletarian subjectivation: 'the process of "becoming a subject" is difficult and confusing, and it is also not clear what it means to think in the way that the subject has to think'. Chehonadskih's brilliant book unravels a forgotten epistemic thread emerging from the material collectivism of the 1920s, one that favours mutualism, perspectivism and comradely cooperation over self-interest and individuality.

Her book is a remarkable contribution not only to the study of early Soviet philosophy but also to ecological theory. It might offer a blueprint for both political action in response to our planetary climate crisis and new ways of thinking and organising knowledge. In the Soviet counter-canon she excavates, thinking is conceptualised as collective and material world-building rather than individual consciousness. This approach reflects a uniquely ecological understanding of cognition, where thinking entwines with activity, and the body with the environment. Feelings and ideas are no longer abstract but somatised within the body, located in the head, throat, stomach, chest and the sexual organs: 'Everyone has an entire imperialism encamped down below', as Platonov aptly put it. From the perspective of feeling, thinking, acting, labouring collectives, political philosophy shifts from analysing hegemony to developing new capacities for sharing and strengthening the weak. An ecology for the proletariat demands an equitable distribution of resources among all the poor in the environment – humans, plants, machines and working-class bears. With Bogdanov in mind, admiring heavy mediaeval armour in a museum, the time to bear the weight of the past may have finally come.

Isabel Jacobs

Knowledge without knowing

Alenka Zupančič, *Disavowal* (Cambridge/Hoboken: Polity Press, 2024). 162pp. £35.00 hb., £9.99 pb., 978 1 50956 119 3 hb., 978 1 50956 120 9 pb.

In 1962, J.G. Ballard's *The Drowned World* gave us an account of the counterproductive tendency of knowledge. When the novel's protagonists are faced with the reality of the climate disaster – that the drowned, scorched Europe will continue to become even more inhospitable – their admission of this destruction paradoxically *inhibits* any effective reaction. As both Kerans and his team become increasingly confronted with their slim chances of success in staving off the impending catastrophe, any acknowledgement of the reality is a simultaneous dismissal of the gravity of the outlook. By agreeing on the disastrous state of the world, their preoccupations shift elsewhere, onto dream-like, existential, and even trivial preoccupations – onto anything, in short, but the reality of the situation itself.

What Ballard reproduces is the tendency of knowledge to be admitted yet simultaneously rejected. It is precisely this predicament which Alenka Zupančič intends to deconstruct in *Disavowal*, showing that this paradox of knowledge applies to the basic coordinates of today's political sphere. For Zupančič, the key to understanding our collective impotence in the face social catastrophe lies in an appropriation of what Freud called *Verleugnung* (disavowal), whereby we *admit* something, but *act* entirely as if the opposite were the case. It is the constitutively self-defeating structure of knowledge which plagues late capitalist society's capacity to effectively deal with its greatest threats: the ecological crisis, nuclear warfare, political corruption and exploitation, etc.

By taking Freud's use of *Verleugnung*, via Octave Mannoni's formula for disavowal ('I know very well but nevertheless …'), and framing it according to its ontological weight as well as its collective (rather than individual-pathological) structure, the robust malleability of contemporary ideology as well as conspiracy theories can be better accounted for. Zupančič's efforts to bridge the ontological and the ideological are undoubtedly impressive, and faithful to the original meaning of the psychoanalytic intervention. It is in part Freud who depicted the permanent entanglement of the constitution of subjectivity and everyday life; a reciprocal movement between an ontological origin and everyday expressions of the unconscious (slips of the tongue, jokes, etc. all reproduce an antagonism at the beginning of subjecthood).

For Freud, fetishism is the first prototype of disavowal: it permits the belief in a non-existent object to persist despite our conscious acknowledgement that this object does not exist. This 'real-imaginary' object is the maternal phallus, the last bulwark against the fact of castration; the accordance of sexuality to 'social' modes of enjoyment. Where the infant initially believes in the existence of the maternal phallus, it does not need to recognise the possible lack of the phallus – that the phallus always implies its own potential non-existence (as Lacan states, that the phallus signifies only its own absence – unlike the penis, which can be reduced to its biological reality, the phallus has an unmistakable symbolic function: its meaning is impersonal and socially formulated, an obscure sign of power that is nevertheless not reducible to the penis itself, and thus a symbol not of presence or virility but absence and impotence). The universality of the phallus, its existence both in men and women, would be a guarantee that the phallus *is what it is*. Yet the traumatic revelation for the infant that the mother has no phallus is in itself the negation of the phallus by itself – a recognition of the precarious state of the phallus.

With a fetish, however, sexuality assumes a reactionary position against this fact of castration. The fetishist may consciously acknowledge the fact of the non-existence of the maternal phallus (of castration, in other words), yet their behaviour implies something else: the fetishist never reaches the point of a sexual relation in which the lack of the phallus is directly encountered. It sets up as the object of its own drive a point which precedes the recognition of the absence of the phallus (such as a foot or a shoe). The fetish is an objectified method of enjoying the *lack* of a sexual relation. Consciously, the fetishist can acknowledge that 'I know very well that the maternal phallus does not exist' yet at the same time the 'but nevertheless' is embodied in their fetish, in the fact that they never materially confront this fact of castration. As Mannoni writes, the fetishist does not need to *utter* the second portion of the formula ('but nevertheless …'), since the fetish is itself this disavowal, this 'but nevertheless …' is embodied in their object choice.

Zupančič's contribution is to pursue Freud's inquiry to show that this mode of relating to inconvenient knowledge – to dismiss it precisely by admitting it – defines not only fetishised individual belief, but ideology as a whole. She builds on the example of the Italian adventurer Giacomo Casanova, who describes his pleasure at manipulating the naivety of others by pretending to be a magician. He is very well aware that his 'magic' is merely performative nonsense, and yet when a storm unexpectedly breaks out during one of his spectacles, he finds himself believing his own performance: he fearfully remains inside a magical chalk circle which according to his mock-narrative would be a magical protection from lightning. In other words, as Zupančič suggests, he 'falls victim to his own magic'. In this double movement of disbelief that sustains belief itself, Casanova utilises castration as a defence *against* castration: the magic that he mocks ('the symbolic narrative of magic is after all nonsense') becomes a tool of protection when the irrationality or threat of this magic is revealed ('yet if I stay in the chalk circle, the magic cannot affect me either way'). By disavowing a direct belief, a mediated, symbolic belief is avowed: 'I know very well that magic and the "chalk circle" is a joke, but I am nevertheless protected by remaining in the chalk circle, even if I do not really believe in it'.

In order to frame this paradox as operating on the ontological level, in the primary register of *being* and *knowing* itself, Zupančič returns to Descartes' *cogito*, and in particular Lacan's problematic reading of it. The *cogito*, the identification of thinking with being, is initially rejected by Lacan where the psychoanalytic subject is concerned – the unconscious is after all where thinking eludes my being. Yet Lacan eventually reverts to his original position, reading the *cogito* as an affirmation of the self-contradictory discrepancy which makes the relation between thinking and being an unconscious relation *par excellence*: the 'thinking act' which registers being is a momentary disruption in knowledge, a momentary abjection in which thought affirms being by a rejection of itself. Hence Lacan's famous variation on Descartes' *cogito ergo sum*:

> I think where I am not, therefore I am where I do not think. I am not whenever I am the plaything of my thought; I think of what I am where I do not think to think.

The ultimate outcome of Descartes' meditations is to reduce thought to an empty formality, to evacuate all *thought content* and in so doing to discover being as the accidental by-product of thought's inability to account for itself. In this sense, Lacan insists that the *cogito* is in fact the subject of the unconscious, one in which being and an 'impossible knowledge' are contracted into an imperceptible singularity, in which, in other words, knowledge is a rejection of being. Knowledge is in this sense itself a fetish, it continues to function insofar as it is disavowed. Its lack of ontological 'weight' becomes the inverted ground upon which it is perpetually justified. Put more simply, knowledge 'functions' by the fact that it simultaneously rejects itself. To have knowledge of a thing is to install a certain screen *against* a recognition of said thing.

Another of Zupančič's examples reveals a similar ability of subjectivity to apprehend finitude (death) by latently rejecting it: a man says to his wife, 'If one of us dies, I shall move to Paris.' The possibility of death is uttered, yet the second part of the statement reveals that if death is possible, it is after all the wife who will be dying. Disavowal operates by a constitutive, yet necessary exclusion; a certain element in our shared subjective register is ejected, and in so doing we can speak in the affirmative about a Symbolic fact whilst at the same time denying its universal or 'true' significance. Consider the manifold examples of forest fires, droughts, floodings, freak weather, etc.; as Zupančič puts it, these very real events seemingly prevent us from recognising the 'Real' upon which they touch – the overarching rupture in day-to-day life that the climate crisis represents. Each isolated recognition of some natural disaster veils a more fundamental comprehension of a universal destruction which lies behind isolated disasters. This is the difference employed by Lacan between reality (in this example, an isolated natural disaster) and the Real (the global warming responsible for these disasters and threatening the basic coordinates of social reality, i.e. the Symbolic). We know these facts only insofar as our true knowledge (a complete knowledge of what they mean) is veiled.

Conspiracy theories are the 'other side' of the same coin on which rational enlightenment thought is located. Descartes' *Meditations*, as Zupančič points out, begin with an almost comical level of paranoia over being deceived. The 'deceiving Other' is what drives Descartes towards the perpetual doubt which culminates in the metaphysical status of the *cogito*. For Zupančič, this same epistemological paranoia, this conviction of a 'deceiving Other' colouring everyday life, returns in the form of conspiracy theories – one of her preferred references being the far-right, 4chan-originated QAnon. Rational scepticism lends itself to an asymmetrical avowal of conspiracy theories (as opposed to 'mainstream' theories): the sceptical attitude initially includes the outlandish claims of conspiracy theories (a generalised scepticism of the mainstream and of conspiracies). Yet the fact that, unlike the mainstream, conspiracies come to reflect in their theories this idea of a deceiving 'big Other', the paranoiac-sceptical, enlightenment subject leans towards them, finds in them an independent knowledge in the absence of the Other, their own political *cogito*.

What is crucial, then, about disavowal is that it explains how we can know something without *actually* knowing it; how we can accept and simultaneously reject something. The strength of Zupančič's argument is to reflect this political tendency in a fundamental ontological tension: the negative relationship between knowledge and being. However, is something not missing in accounting for political/social behaviour by the function of disavowal? The doctrine of disavowal can ultimately be summarised as follows: we *know* only so that we can continue being ignorant. We disavow something in order to continue enjoying it. If enjoyment really is the *raison d'être* of disavowal, ought we not to problematise this same enjoyment as much as we have dissected knowledge?

Zupančič's model presupposes a self-serving enjoyment, where disavowal furnishes a continued (ignorant) pleasure. Here we should remember one of Freud's crucial discoveries: enjoyment must also be located *beyond the pleasure principle*. Enjoyment is constructed in the impasses of the social, and can as such directly contradict pleasure; collective enjoyment is generated in the face of the failure of personal enjoyment.

To understand this, we can return to *The Drowned World*. Interestingly, the paradoxical reaction of the protagonists – to stay and likely perish in former London as the rest of the research team moves further North – cannot be explained via the pleasure principle. No longer simply contending with insufferable temperatures and Earth returning to prehistoric conditions, the survivors additionally face their own psychological self-destructiveness. Collective nightmares, hallucinations and archetypal images of mankind's parasitic relation to nature plague them far more than the ecological threat, yet encourage them to stay out of an aestheticised, narrative-form of what can best be described as the Freudian death drive. Their decision to stay is not a disavowal in the name of a protracted enjoyment. It is rather a drive serving an imaginary horror *more horrifying* than their reality itself.

It is precisely this self-contradictory centre of enjoyment – its existence beyond the pleasure principle in the realm of the death drive – that disavowal alone misses. Where Zupančič's exploration of disavowal centres around the mediated 'use' of pleasure (to adapt Foucault's term), it misses the impersonal, anti-individualistic colour of ideology. Enjoyment transgresses the biological coordinates of pleasure – enjoyment is not only located beyond the finitude of the individual, but beyond any determinate aim or determinate object relation. This is one of Freud's principal theses in *Beyond the Pleasure Principle*, a thesis which is even more clearly furnished by Laplanche's (and to an extent Lacan's) reading of Freud. We enjoy abstractly, without any stable formula of enjoyment, divorced from the specific thing which we claim to enjoy – since this thing itself does not exist. Enjoyment is constructed on the ground of a non-relation (a 'lack' in Lacanian terms), and thus persists only by relinquishing any immediate pleasure.

The death drive signifies an enjoyment that denies pleasure, denies life. For example, the traumatic realisation of the absence of the maternal phallus, the recognition that castration is immanent, and that free, individualised desire is impossible. The coordinates, in other words, in which fetishism emerges – these events are not pleasurable, and yet lay the ground for an excessive, destructive enjoyment. Fetishist enjoyment turns away from life and towards death: an enjoyment (e.g. of a shoe) that counters reproduction.

What Zupančič fails to consider is an enjoyment that rejects pleasure (the pleasure in continuing to live as if 'everything is okay'). Deleuze's understanding of habit becomes relevant here: habit is a formal mode of constructing 'sense' by grounding what is repeated through the very act of repeating it. Habit is, according to this definition, a political factor: it is often not with a direct avowal, but with a retroactive justification, that political formations arise. It is by acting first, and grounding the intention of this act after, that we can persistently drive ourselves towards catastrophe. Repetition justifies itself – it is not the thing being repeated, but the principle of repetition itself.

Disavowal as a 'knowledge that does not know itself' is an important political factor. Although it has been more popularised by Žižek, Zupančič remains faithful to its conceptual origin (discussing its implication for Freud and Mannoni) whilst impressively constructing her argument in accordance with the ontological categories of knowledge and being, thereby grounding disavowal as a social-ontological function in a way which eludes Žižek's discussions of the concept. Yet disavowal obscures a more impersonal political factor: a habitual-destructive enjoyment beyond the pleasure principle.

In order to approach today's dominant political antagonisms, the image of humanity as acting in the service of individualistic pleasure must be abandoned. The perceived 'self-sacrifice' of QAnon and related conspiracy theories, the desolate world-outlook of reactionary populism including its performative animation in Trump, and even the formless indifference with which liberal democracies support an increasingly exploitative and destructive techno-capitalism, reveal an ideological movement unaccounted for by pleasure alone. The colour of the contemporary political landscape is one in which a psychology of pleasure – under which disavowal can be subsumed – is insufficient. What should be stressed is the political dimension of the death drive, of an impersonal, pleasure-less enjoyment which retroactively formulates what it is repeating.

Rafael Holmberg

Perpetually thinking beyond

Yuk Hui, *Machine and Sovereignty: For a Planetary Thinking* (Minneapolis: University of Minnesota Press, 2024). 368pp., £23.99 pb., 978 1 51791 741 8

When did the awareness of living on a planet first start to emerge? This is a difficult question since its various implications did not all arrive in the same time and place. Ideas of a spherical Earth and heliocentrism can be traced back at least to the writings of Ancient Greece. But the likes of Aristarchus of Samos would have been unable to conceive of the Copernican trauma that now underlies the profane image of Planet Earth revealed by modern astronomy, 150 million kilometres from the sun, awaiting solar death 5 billion years in the future. Nor would

Copernicus, Galileo or Bruno have been able to foresee the increasing technological transformations of Earth and its inhabitants.

It is common now to hear that human societies are technologically determined, that technology is akin to an alien force rewriting human nature and that artificial technology will lead to catastrophic wars or even the end of humanity. We can think of the reaction of Martin Heidegger when he first saw the images of Earth made possible by the emerging technologies of space exploration and satellite imaging, declaring that Western metaphysics had culminated in cybernetics and that 'only a God can save us'. We can only imagine what he would say of our current situation, in which many consider his warnings to have come to fruition.

It is this situation which Yuk Hui tackles in his recent work, *Machine and Sovereignty*, envisioned as the third volume in a series comprising *Recursivity and Contingency* (2019) and *Art and Cosmotechnics* (2021). This recent work brings his excursion within the philosophy of technology into contact with political philosophy. These two domains, he argues, can no longer be thought in separation and he describes this work as a first attempt at writing a *Tractatus Politico-Technologicus*. The ultimate goal Hui sets himself is to imagine the conditions for peaceful and harmonious modes of life at the planetary scale through an embrace of cybernetics.

Unlike Heidegger, Hui is not fatally pessimistic about the potentials of cybernetics, which he argues is often uncritically reduced to 'surveillance capitalism or societies of control'. Rather, Hui contends that new political possibilities can be opened through a reconceptualisation of technology and he seeks to understand how cybernetics can become the basis for 'planetary happiness', a notion he likens to Kant's idea of 'perpetual peace', which is the telos of what Hui terms 'planetary thinking':

> To think planetarily, first of all, means thinking beyond the configuration of modern nation-states, which have not been able to move away from vicious economic and military competition; second, it means formulating a language of coexistence that will allow diverse people and species to live on the same planet; and third, developing a new framework that will enable us to go beyond the question of territory, respond to the current ecological crisis, and reverse the accelerated entropic process of the Anthropocene.

Alongside Heidegger, Hui engages with a wide range of thinkers who engage with the philosophy of technology, ranging from Lewis Mumford, Gilbert Simondon and André Leroi-Gourhan to Bruno Latour and his mentor Bernard Stiegler. He also draws liberally on wider philosophy, including at times Chinese philosophers, although he is primarily concerned with critiquing and overcoming the limits of the Western philosophical tradition and its conceptualisation of an all consuming *technic*, which has animated his previous expositions of 'cosmotechnics' and 'technodiversity'. Yet, in line with his intention to embrace the political dimensions of technology, the book is largely centred around his engagement with Hegel and Schmitt, who both rejected Kant's vision of a 'world republic' and who figure respectively as the thinkers of the nation-state and the *Großräume*.

A key concept that underlies Hui's exploration of political philosophy is 'political epistemology'. Hui argues that distinct political epistemologies emerge to justify the different iterations of the Mumfordian megamachine as it evolves and develops. The most prominent examples of political epistemologies are 'mechanism' and 'organicism', with Kant's organicism in *The Critique of Judgement* figuring as the critical rupture between prior mechanistic philosophies and the organistic understanding of thinkers like Hegel. For Hui, the machine and the organism are not simply metaphors but serve as 'ideal models of human society' which can emerge within all aspects of existence. However, in line with wider attitudes to the binary logic of modernity, Hui argues that the dichotomy of mechanism-organicism has been overcome by the cybernetics of modern technology.

The first three chapters are dedicated to Hegel. Hui identifies 'world spirit' as a form of planetary thinking, exploring how Hegel's philosophy can track and explain the emergence of planetary self-awareness through its synchronisation of all distinct civilisations and cultures into a single world history. At the same time, he criticises the limitations of Hegel's Eurocentrism and turns to the work of Georgescu-Roegen on 'bioeconomy' to remedy the absence of entropy and other ecological limitations within Hegel's dialectical framework.

Hegel is described on numerous occasions as a prototypical thinker of cybernetics, with 'dialectics' and 'reflection' being likened respectively to 'recursivity' and 'feedback'. Hegel's logic is not depicted as a romanticist analogy of the organic, but is organicist because of its openness to individuation and contingency, with Hui likening it to 'a monster capable of engulfing every form of existence'. The works of Teillhard de Chardin and Lovelock are described as having continued this Hegelianesque cybernetics, both having positioned the evolution of intelligence within a more explicitly planetary-cybernetic model. Hui's central interest lies in determining how these Hegelian cybernetic tendencies might ultimately surpass Hegel's own state-centric vision articulated in the *Philosophy of Right*.

Hui's main point of criticism concerns Hegel's claim that the freedom of the world spirit culminates in a global order comprised of distinct and divided nation-states. For Hegel, 'there is an organicity of the state but no organicity among the states', a limitation which Hui strongly opposes in his search for a political form adequate to planetary happiness. In chapter six he discusses two possible 'paths' for cybernetic evolution: the 'perfection' of the nation-state system through artificial intelligence or the the construction of a 'digital earth' which brings forth some new political form beyond Hegel's organismic state.

It is attempting to determine what this new political form might be which draws Hui towards Schmitt.

The fourth and fifth chapters investigate the thought of Schmitt. As with Hegel, Hui seeks to draw upon Schmitt's own conceptualisations to go beyond his conclusions. He first critiques the Christian bias of Schmitt's 'political theology', arguing that political epistemology is a better tool for understanding the current political forms which should not be reduced to a Western perspective. Hui then affirms that Schmitt's accomplishment was his overcoming of the mechanism-organicism binary within his theory of 'decisionism'. Also termed 'political vitalism', decisionism disrupts the automation of the state through the sovereign's decision over the state of exception, which figures as the vital force of the state.

Schmitt therefore provides a conceptual basis to imagine how the state of exception could resist a homogenising technologisation of the planet in favour of 'technodiversity'. Hui is attracted by Schmitt's understanding of technology and sovereignty and his desire for plurality, but he is simultaneously opposed to Schmitt's Nazism, his state-centric conceptualisation of the political and the foundational role enmity plays in the political form of the *Großräume*.

Hui argues that Schmitt's *Großräume* is insufficient to ensure true plurality in response to the homogenisation underlying the new spatial revolution of 'digital earth', whereby the megamachine and sovereignty are no longer bounded by the form of the state, proposing that 'true plurality' requires another political epistemology as its foundation, that of 'organology'. This is a term originally used by Canguilhem in relation to Bergson's *Creative Evolution* and inherited by Simondon and Steigler. It was previously discussed by Hui in *Recursivity and Contingency* and is about the overcoming of the boundary between humanity and machines. As the focus of the sixth chapter, it functions as an 'alternative way to understand the relation between the state and technology', one opposed to technological determinism.

Hui ultimately positions technodiversity alongside biodiversity and noodiversity as part of a framework for planetary thinking, with diversity seeming to figure as both a political ideal and practical means of resisting entropy, within which he argues that the 'question of diversity has to be thought of fundamentally from the perspective of technology.' His concern is with how an organological conception of technology can lead to the necessary political forms, beyond the nation-state and the *Großräume*, to ensure such diversity.

In the final chapter, we find an elaboration and final discussion of how a planetary thinking framed by biodiversity, noodiversity and technodiversity can open up new possibilities outside of homogenising universalism, geopolitical hostility and technological determinism. Hui proposes 'epistemological diplomacy' as a basis for 'new forms of communication beyond the state' which would ensure the heterogeneity of localities. It remains somewhat underdeveloped, but he envisions it as superseding the current modes of diplomacy focused on economic and militaristic matters, towards the 'development of programs that might facilitate the development of technodiversity, noodiversity, and biodiversity.'

He aligns his vision with Kant's world republic, and also its recent reformulation by Karatani in *Structures of World History*, whom he agrees with in spirit if not in detail. Hui wants to imagine a planet beyond military and economic aggression, beyond the state and the market, in which technology, humanity and ecology can all flourish in diverse ways.

However, if one expects any clear and practical proposals then the final chapter will be disappointing. In concrete terms, it is much easier for Hui to tell us what his vision of planetary happiness does not consist of and at times it is easy to wonder if any substantial insights undergird all the neologisms and philosophical references. He can only approach planetary thinking in the most abstract terms, a world where organic diversity and mechanical production proliferate symbiotically and humanity has overcome competition and warfare without being subsumed into some homogenised universal.

In the sixth chapter he opens up a discussion concerning Bergson and mysticism, referring to it as 'a much larger and more powerful force capable of deploying mechanism for its own service.' He also equates it with the Bergsonian term 'attachment to life' and positions it as a 'deviation from the homogeneity of mechanization and a movement toward the new vocation of machines.' From Bergson he also adopts the language of spiritualisation and part of his argument in the final chapter is that 'the spiritualization of matter has to take place by contesting the homogenization of digital technology that has been solely guided by speed and efficiency.'

Hence, whilst Hui's thinking is engagingly erudite, comprehensive and provocative, the reader will wonder what it would take for his abstract vision to truly become concretised. While the monotheistic bias of Heidegger might not befit Hui's cosmological stance, are we still desperately awaiting some divine power to set our Spaceship Earth on the right course? It is hard to escape this question, but Hui's turn to the mystical can also be seen as his attempt to dislocate his project from any homogenising rationality, to open up a space for what his occasional interlocutor, Viveiros de Castro, might term 'ontological anarchism', and hence to immanentise the negentropic possibilities of diversification.

Hui has become an increasingly influential philosophical voice concerning the question of technology and in this pursuit of its political dimensions there is much to engage with. While Hui cannot himself depict the future of planetary happiness in detail, the fact that he has not given up on it is undoubtedly a good sign. His work is a noble step towards the uncovering of regulative principles which could guide the development of a cybernetic planet beyond the current horizons of devastating warfare, economic uncertainty and ecological collapse, towards more bountiful, harmonious and spiritual possibilities. Whether such a planet can ever actualise, remains, perhaps perpetually, to be seen.

Connor Eckersall

www.ingramcontent.com/pod-product-compliance
Lightning Source LLC
Chambersburg PA
CBHW080230100526
44584CB00022BA/3189